Mazda MX-5

MAINTENANCE AND UPGRADES MANUAL

Mazda MX-5

Rob Hawkins

THE CROWOOD PRESS

First published in 2017 by
The Crowood Press Ltd
Ramsbury, Marlborough
Wiltshire SN8 2HR

www.crowood.com

British Library Cataloguing-in-Publication Data
A catalogue record for this book is available from the British Library.

ISBN 978 1 78500 282 3

Disclaimer
Safety is of the utmost importance in every aspect of an automotive workshop. The practical
procedures and the tools and equipment used in automotive workshops are potentially
dangerous. Tools should be used in strict accordance with the manufacturer's recommended
procedures and current health and safety regulations. The author and publisher cannot accept
responsibility for any accident or injury caused by following the advice given in this book.

Acknowledgements
Rob Hawkins would like to thank MJ Motors of Birstall in Batley for selling him his first MX-5 and
helping to maintain and repair it; Roadrunner Racing of Hull for workshop time and testing
various products; Peter Jones at MazMania for help with hoods; Noisekiller for soundproofing
expertise; Stuart Mills of MEV for the use of his test track; Ewens Sports Cars (Fengate MOT,
Peterborough) for assistance with fitting guides; Alonze Custom Fabrication for showing how
to widen steel wheels; Leather Revive for refurbishing seats and Blueprint, Hammerite, KYB
Dampers, David Manners Group, K&N, Powerflex and Frost Restoration for the supply of parts.

Typeset by Jean Cussons Typesetting, Diss, Norfolk

Printed and bound in Malaysia by Times Offset (M) Sdn Bhd

contents

tools and safety

POPULAR TOOLS

Japanese-manufactured cars, such as the Mazda MX-5, are constructed with a small range of metric fastenings, the most common requiring a selection of 10mm, 12mm, 14mm and 17mm spanners and sockets. Unlike many other cars from around the world that use 13mm or ½in fastenings, the Japanese have largely avoided this superstitious size.

So most jobs can be tackled with the aforementioned spanners and sockets (there are a few 19–27mm fittings

as well), along with an assortment of screwdrivers, a few Allen keys and a collection of persuasive implements, such as hammers and pry bars.

The list of desired tools can easily expand, however, depending on how involved you want to get with fixing, maintaining and modifying an MX-5. Any work on the suspension or brakes will usually require a trolley jack and axle stands, and it's important to know where to position them (*see* later in this chapter for more details). A breaker bar comes in handy to undo the wheel bolts and any fittings that require extra leverage.

Most tools are concerned with undoing fastenings or removing parts. However, there is also a selection of tools that help with ensuring parts are correctly fitted, one of the most useful being a torque wrench. These can be quite cheap, at around £25, and ensure important fittings such as wheel bolts are correctly tightened.

AVOIDING ACCIDENTS

This book provides many step-by-step guides to help show how to repair or modify an MX-5 using tools that can be dangerous if they are operated incorrectly. For example, an electric drill can slip and slice through skin or the panels of your MX-5. Sparks from an angle grinder can set fire to upholstery, damage glass or even damage your eyes if you don't wear protective goggles. Nuts and bolts that are not

A torque wrench ensures important fittings are correctly tightened.

Always wear suitable goggles and gloves when using an angle grinder to help protect yourself from hot sparks and debris.

fully tightened can loosen and result in an accident, such as a road wheel that falls off.

When following the instructions in this book, be aware of the safety aspects of the work involved and do not rush any of the tasks that are outlined. If you are at all unsure about any of the information covered, seek further advice before proceeding.

Some of the tools covered in this book require protective clothing to be worn when using them, and parts of the MX-5 may also need to be protected. For instance, when using an angle grinder, metal sparks and debris will fly in all directions, so make sure you are wearing a suitable pair of goggles and thick gloves and most of your body is covered in clothing to avoid being burnt by the hot sparks that are

created. Grinding sparks can also damage the MX-5, especially glass and upholstery, so protect it with thick blankets or cardboard.

If you need to weld, the same rules apply as when using an angle grinder, except you will need a suitable welding mask to avoid damaging your eyes – also make sure there is nobody nearby who could look at the light created when welding and potentially damage their eyesight.

When using an electric drill, wear goggles to prevent debris from the drill hitting your eyes. Make sure you use the correct drill bits for the job and don't forget they can get hot after drilling.

Do not take shortcuts when working on your MX-5. It may save time, but accidents can be fatal. One of the most

Drive-on wheel ramps are useful for securely raising the front or rear of the MX-5 to allow you to work underneath it.

When raising a front corner, the chassis leg may be stronger than the jacking point.

Never rely upon a trolley jack to raise and support the vehicle; always use at least one axle stand.

The rear of the MX-5 can be raised via the differential, then supported along the back of the sills with axle stands.

common mistakes and cause of many accidents is raising the vehicle with a trolley jack to either remove a road wheel or work underneath it. First, make sure the vehicle is on level ground and that at least one of the wheels that will remain on the floor is chocked with a block of wood or a brick. If one of the rear wheels remains on the floor, apply the handbrake and select first gear for manual gearboxes, or park for automatics.

When raising the vehicle with a trolley jack or similar device (bottle jack or scissor jack for instance), position it under a jacking point or chassis leg, but make sure this area is solid and not heavily corroded. If the area is infested with corrosion, the jack could collapse and fall over if the metalwork breaks up when supporting the weight of the vehicle. So always check the condition of the jacking point first. The MX-5's jacking points are along the sills, but the metal can become weakened here and start to bend, so it may be better to feed a trolley jack further underneath and raise the car underneath a chassis leg instead.

When raising the rear of the MX-5, it is possible to position a trolley jack underneath the differential.

After raising a corner of the car or the rear of it, always support it with at least one axle stand. Never rely upon any type of jack to keep a car raised and secure. This is very important, and whilst it takes a minute or two more to find a suitable position for the axle stand, it can save your life.

STICKY WHEELS

Alloy road wheels can sometimes stick to the cast iron wheel hubs, making them difficult to remove once the wheel bolts have been undone. If this happens, make sure the vehicle is raised and secured with at least once axle stand, then position a long, thick length of wood against the back of the wheel rim and hit it with a large lump hammer to help release it. Apply a smear of copper grease to the mating surface of the wheel and hub (not the brakes) to reduce the risk of this happening again.

Alloy road wheels can stick on to the hub, but make sure the car is raised and securely supported before attempting to remove the road wheel.

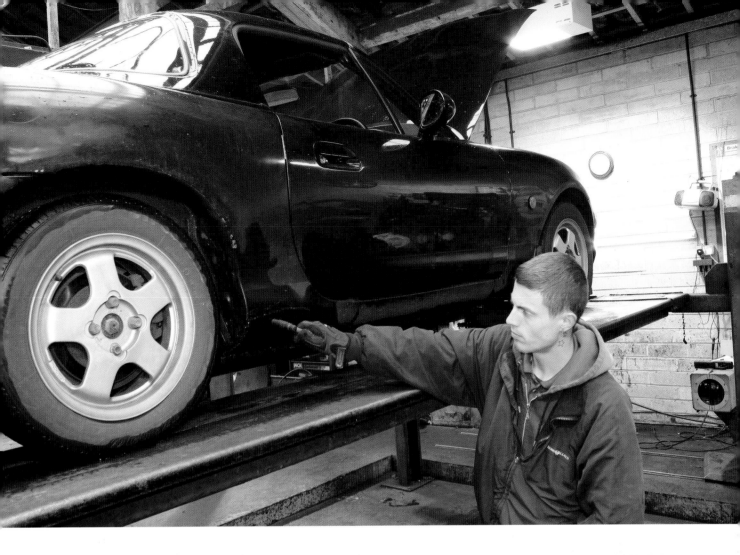

routine checks

EVERY WEEK

With the MX-5 parked on level ground and the engine cold, it takes a matter of minutes to check the fluid levels under the bonnet, the tyres and the lights.

Fluid Levels

From underneath the bonnet, extract the engine oil dipstick found at the back of the engine bay, wipe the end with a clean cloth, then carefully reinsert it fully and pull it back out again. There should be some oil on the end of the dipstick and markers showing the minimum and maximum levels. There's roughly 800ml difference between the minimum marker and the maximum marker. So if the oil needs topping up, calculate how much is needed based on this figure. The recommended oil for the engine (1.6- and 1.8-litre) is a 10W40 semi-synthetic or synthetic oil to ACEA A3/B4 specification.

Elsewhere in the engine bay, the brake fluid level can be checked via the reservoir. This is located at the back of the engine bay in front of the driver's seat. The reservoir is a clear container, so the level can be checked without having

to release the cap – look for the minimum and maximum markings on the outside. If you need to top up the brake fluid, clean around the reservoir first to avoid dirt getting inside. Top up with a DOT 4-rated brake fluid. Avoid spilling this fluid on to any painted surface because it will strip the paint off it.

There's 800ml between the maximum and minimum markers on the engine oil dipstick, so avoid over-filling when topping up.

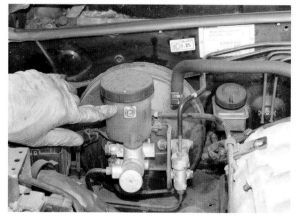

The level in the brake fluid reservoir can be checked without having to remove the cap.

The clutch fluid reservoir is next to the brake fluid reservoir and uses the same DOT 4 fluid.

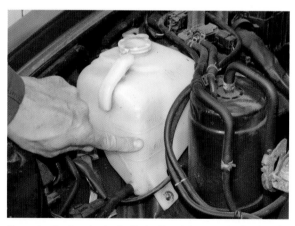

The coolant level can be checked by looking at the expansion bottle. Make sure the level is between the low and full markings.

The clutch fluid reservoir also needs to be checked and uses the same DOT 4-rated fluid as the brake fluid. This is located next to the brake fluid reservoir and is a smaller reservoir.

The coolant level is very straightforward to check via the expansion tank that's fitted onto the offside inner wing of the engine bay (driver's side for RHD cars). It's a clear plastic container with markings for maximum and minimum levels. The engine should be cold when checking the level.

If it needs topping up, unclip the cap on the top of the expansion tank, then add a mixture of water and antifreeze before refitting the cap.

The power steering fluid level isn't quite as straightforward to check as the coolant. The reservoir is located in front of the air filter box, close to the right side of the radiator (when looking from the front of the engine bay). It's a small, round, black container, so you cannot see the fluid level without unscrewing the cap on the top of it. Once unscrewed, extract the cap and clean the dipstick on the underside of it. Reinsert the dipstick but do not screw the cap back on. Extract the dipstick and check the level – it should be between the H mark for high and the L mark for low. If the power steering fluid needs topping up, carefully add a small quantity of Dexron II and check the level again.

The final fluid level to check underneath the bonnet is for the windscreen washer fluid. This is located to the rear of the air filter box when looking from the front of the engine bay. It's a clear container, so it should be easy to check the level visually and top it up if necessary. Do not add washing up liquid to the windscreen washer bottle because it can congeal and block the pipework and filters. Instead, add a mixture of water and screen wash or use pre-diluted screen wash.

Do not screw the dipstick and cap fully in when checking the power steering fluid level in the reservoir.

The windscreen washer reservoir is located behind the air filter box, or in this case, an open cone aftermarket air filter.

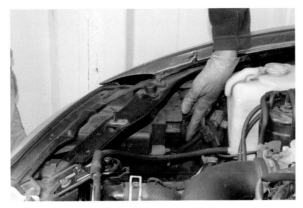

The headlight bulbs on the Mk2 MX-5 can be awkward to access from within the engine bay.

The rear light unit on the Mk2 MX-5 is secured with two 10mm nuts and one crosshead screw.

Lights

Few people check all of the exterior lighting is working properly, but this should be routinely inspected. Fortunately, lighting such as indicators is checked every time you use it – if the indicators flash too quickly then a bulb isn't working. However, a blown headlight bulb or a lack of brake lights are not so easy to spot, but only take a few seconds to check. When reversing up to a car, building or into a garage, press the brake pedal to check both brake lights illuminate. The same quick test can be conducted at the front for the headlights, simply switch them on with the car parked, then take a look.

Some blown bulbs are not so quick to replace. On the Mk1 MX-5, the pop-up headlight unit has to be removed, which involves undoing a series of screws at the front and side. On the Mk2 the bulbs are accessed via the engine bay.

If you are renewing a halogen bulb, avoid touching the glass – grease from your fingers can contaminate and overheat the bulb.

Rear bulbs on the Mk1 MX-5 are straightforward to change – they are accessed from inside the boot. The rear indicator bulb requires the holder to be removed, whereas the other bulbs require a bulb holder assembly to be unclipped.

On the Mk2, undo two 10mm nuts from inside the boot and one crosshead screw on top of the rear light unit to release it from the back of the car. It's quite a tight fit, so will need manoeuvring a little to help release it. Once removed, the bulb holders for the rear light unit can be twisted anti-clockwise to release them and renew a bulb.

Tyres

Finally, the tyres should be routinely checked every week, so invest in an accurate pressure gauge and spend a few minutes checking the tyre pressures. This also gives you the chance to look at the sidewalls for damage and the tread for excessive or uneven wear. The tyres are the only components on the car that ensure you stay on the road, so they are extremely important and should be meticulously maintained.

Don't assume the tyre pressures are fine so long as the tyres are not flat. Check them every week.

Washing the Car

Washing the car is an important aspect of routine maintenance. It not only keeps the bodywork clean, it helps to remove dirt that can damage the paintwork and is a good opportunity to inspect the condition of the paintwork. The wheels, for instance, can quickly start to corrode from road salt, brake dust and other dirt, so wash them thoroughly with a sponge or brush, then use a small quantity of wheel cleaner to remove any stubborn dirt.

In some cases, washing the MX-5 won't help keep the paintwork looking clean and shiny, especially on older cars where the paintwork has faded. Sometimes this can be rescued with polish or a more abrasive T-cut.

TWICE A YEAR

Many aspects of routine maintenance are outlined in depth throughout this book, so the following section provides a brief checklist.

Drivebelts

Assuming you are already conducting the weekly checks outlined above, one area of the engine that should be checked at least twice a year is the auxiliary drivebelts. There are two of them and they are located at the front of the engine bay. They drive the water pump, alternator and power steering pump (and the air conditioning pump if fitted), using the power from the crankshaft pulley. The tension on these belts should be checked to ensure they are not too slack or too tight. If a belt is too tight, it can damage the bearings of the components they are connected to – a common cause of water pump failure. If they are too slack, the belt can slip, resulting in problems such as the engine running hot and the alternator not being able to fully recharge the battery. A slipping belt will also overheat and eventually fail.

Checking the tension on the drivebelts takes a few seconds. With the engine switched off, try to twist the belt. It should be possible to twist it by a quarter of a turn, neither

Washing the wheels once a week ensures they remain clean and that road salt and dirt doesn't damage the finish.

Paintwork that has faded can sometimes be rescued with a thorough polish.

Twist the belt to check its tension. It should be possible to twist it by a quarter of a turn.

Renew the radiator cap if you are unsure of its age.

more nor less. Adjusting the tension on the belt is covered in the next chapter under drivebelt renewal.

Radiator

The coolant level should be checked weekly by inspecting the level in the expansion tank, but it's also worthwhile releasing the pressure cap on the top of the radiator (only when the engine is cold) to look inside and make sure the coolant level is up to the top. If the pipe between the plastic expansion tank and the radiator becomes blocked, the coolant level in the expansion tank may look fine but the radiator could be empty, which can result in overheating. Similarly, if you do not know the age of the radiator cap, renew it. The cap maintains pressure in the cooling system, so fit a new one to ensure it's working properly.

Air Filter

The condition of the air filter can be quickly checked and any dirt removed to help improve engine breathing. A dirty air filter restricts airflow, increases fuel consumption and can reduce engine performance. The air filter is contained in a plastic box on the right side of the engine bay when looking from the front of the car. Undo any metal clips to release the lid and look inside. If a standard air filter is fitted, remove it and inspect the condition of it, removing any dirt. Use a vacuum cleaner to remove any dirt from inside the air filter box. If the air filter is dirty or you don't know when it was last changed, it may be worthwhile renewing it.

Windscreen Wipers

The windscreen wipers are usually checked automatically whenever they are needed to clean the windscreen, but it's also worth running a finger along the rubber blades to make sure they haven't split. Wiper blades are cheap to renew and straightforward to fit.

Brakes

Routine servicing of the brakes is covered in depth in Chapter 6, but there are a few quick checks that can be conducted. If you can see the brake discs through the wheels,

shine a torch to inspect their condition. Look for fractures and excessive wear of the disc (a lip will appear around the outer edge).

Take the car for a drive and try not to brake, then stop the car and place a hand near each brake to see if any of them are hot, indicating that the brake is binding (*see* Chapter 6 for how to fix this problem). Do not touch a hot brake disc as it could burn your skin. If you have an infrared thermometer, this is a safer and more accurate method of measuring the temperature of each brake disc.

The road wheels should be removed at least once a year to inspect the brakes. This is when you will probably discover that most MX-5 alloy wheels stick on to the hubs. A

Shine a torch through the wheels to inspect the condition of the brake disc visually.

A little copper grease on the mating surfaces of the hub and road wheel helps to reduce the risk of the wheel seizing onto the hub in the future.

solution to this problem is outlined in Chapter 1, but as a matter of precaution, always smear a little copper grease on the mating surface of the road wheel and the hub to help reduce the risk of this problem recurring (do not apply copper grease to the braking surface of the brake disc).

Wheel Nuts

The wheel nuts must be securely fitted and should be periodically checked (every six months). A torque wrench is the most accurate means of ensuring the wheel nuts are sufficiently tight – they should be tightened to 110Nm.

Preventing Water Damage

Water is a major problem for the MX-5 because it can get inside the bodywork and cause corrosion. Thankfully it is a small car and there are only a few areas to check to see if they are waterlogged. Starting in the boot, remove the carpet and spare wheel to look for water in the spare wheel well and inside the battery area (and the opposite side as well). If water has collected, it may be possible to release a rubber drain plug and allow it to escape, or wipe it up with clean cloths. If water has collected inside the battery compartment, it's worth removing the battery to dry the area and check for corrosion.

Inside the cabin, check the carpets are not wet. If they

are, dry them and try to trace the cause of the water leak. It may be a collapsed door or hood seal or damage to the hood, for example.

The sills are known to corrode on the MX-5, so make sure they can drain any water that escapes into them. There are small drain holes along the underside, which should be routinely cleaned through with a small screwdriver. Each drain hole is merely a tiny gap where the outer sill meets the floor section, so it can easily become blocked with dirt.

BEFORE THE MOT TEST

The annual MOT test can be a nail-biting experience for an old MX-5. Corrosion is one of the biggest threats, so it's important to inspect the car regularly and know where any rust is emerging. Don't be afraid to tap a small hammer or blunt screwdriver along the underside of each sill to check for corrosion. At the rear, waggle the exhaust tailpipe (make sure it's cold) to ensure it's secure and it hasn't corroded (they can break off).

All of the routine checks outlined in this chapter will help with the MOT test, and there are a few more that are quick to conduct. Make sure the doors can be opened from the inside and outside. Check the driver's seat can slide forwards and backwards and lock in position. Switch on the ignition and make sure all the warning lights (for ABS, for example) illuminate and then go out.

Water has collected underneath the battery here, so remove the battery, dry the area and rust protect the metalwork.

Poke a small screwdriver through the sill drain holes to keep them clear and to help drain water out.

Waggle the end of the exhaust when it's cold to check this area of the exhaust system is securely fitted.

The ABS light has remained illuminated here indicating that there's a problem, which will fail the MOT test.

engine maintenance

HOW TO CHANGE THE ENGINE OIL

The oil in the engine can be drained via a sump plug on the underside, which can in theory be accessed without having to raise the vehicle. However, space is tight, so you'll need a shallow container that can hold up to 5 litres of liquid to drain and collect the oil. If your container cannot hold 5 litres but is sufficiently shallow to fit underneath the car, then it is possible to drain the oil until the container is almost full and then refit the sump plug; you can then dispose of the oil then bring back the empty container to finish the job.

If you intend to drain the engine oil without raising the vehicle, then accessing the engine oil drain plug can be just as hard as finding a suitable drain tray. There's room to manoeuvre a socket and ratchet into position, but not enough space to turn it to slacken the drain plug. Use a selection of extension bars to help assemble something long enough to enable a ratchet to be used on the outside of the car.

While draining the engine oil is fiddly, removing the spin-on oil filter can be harder. It's located underneath the inlet manifold, so can be accessed from inside the engine bay. There's enough space to manoeuvre an oil filter strap wrench into position, but often very little room to undo it because of a steady bar bracket that's fitted between the inlet manifold and the bodywork. This steady bar is used to prevent unwanted vibration of the inlet manifold, especially on tickover, which can result in lumpy idling. It can be removed to help provide more room to undo and remove the oil filter. Once you have more space, you may find you will need it if the oil filter is a tight fit. It should only be fitted by hand, but if it has been over-tightened, you might need a chain-type oil filter wrench to grip and undo it. This can result in the old oil filter being slightly crushed around the sides.

TOOLBOX

◆ **Drain tray**
◆ **Ratchet with long extension bars**
◆ **Oil filter strap wrench**
◆ **5 litres of 10W40 semi-synthetic oil**
◆ **Spin-on oil filter**
◆ **Sockets: 10–19mm**

Time: 20 minutes
On your own? Yes

1. Access to the 17mm or 19mm engine oil drain plug is tight with the MX-5 on the ground and space to turn a ratchet is limited. Several long extension bars allow a ratchet to be fitted away from the car so there's more leverage.

2. With low ground clearance, squeezing a standard oil drain tray underneath the MX-5 is impossible. Instead, this old photographic printing tray is sufficiently shallow but can only hold a couple of litres.

3. The MX-5 engine holds around 5 litres of oil, so if you are using a shallow tray that holds less than this amount, the engine oil will need to be drained off in stages, refitting the sump plug each time.

4. Space may be tight for accessing the oil filter from within the engine bay. There's sufficient room to manoeuvre a filter wrench into position, but probably not enough space to turn it.

5. An alloy steady bar that's connected to the inlet manifold can be removed to allow more room to undo and remove the oil filter. It's usually secured in position with 12mm or 14mm bolts.

6. With the steady bar removed, there's a lot more room to unscrew the oil filter, but if it's a tight fit, be prepared to crush it with a chain-type filter strap wrench.

7. The oil filter sits in a horizontal position, so part fill it with fresh oil before fitting it. Also, smear the rubber seal with oil to help prevent it from dragging and tearing when fitting the filter.

8. Check your user manual for the recommended engine oil and quantity. On the Mk2 MX-5 shown here, it's 5 litres of 10W40 semi-synthetic oil. Check the reading on the dipstick, then run the engine and look for leaks.

SPARK PLUG RENEWAL

MX-5 engines are known to develop ignition problems, which are often caused by the HT leads breaking down. While they can be tested, if you are unsure of the age of your HT leads, it's worthwhile renewing them as a full set for peace of mind. The HT leads are connected to the coil pack at the back of the engine bay and each of the four spark plugs on the top of the engine. Replace one HT lead at a time to avoid fitting them onto the wrong connections on the coil pack. The HT leads are all different lengths, so make sure each lead is replaced with one of the same length. Detaching the ends of the HT leads from the spark plugs can be quite difficult. If the old HT leads are brittle, they may break off, leaving the remains attached to the top of the spark plug, so carefully lever off the end of the lead with a screwdriver or trim tool.

While you are renewing the HT leads, you can also remove and inspect the spark plugs. Some makes of spark plug last for up to 100,000 miles, such as Denso's Long Life range, whereas others need to be renewed at shorter intervals. Extract each spark plug with a suitable spark plug socket that includes a rubber insert. When refitting the new spark plug, the rubber insert inside the spark plug socket can sometimes be pulled out, leaving it stuck on the top of the spark plug that has been fitted. The only solution then is to remove the spark plug to retrieve the rubber insert. If

Denso's Long Life spark plugs are intended to last for 100,000 miles.

this happens, try next time using a short length of rubber hose (8–10mm in diameter) to lower the spark plug down into the top of the engine and turn it a few threads. Once in position, you can then finish off with the spark plug socket, and if desired, remove the rubber insert to avoid the risk of losing it again.

Spark plugs should not be over-tightened when fitted because this can damage the thread in the top of the engine (cylinder head). Use a short ⅜in ratchet to hand tighten each spark plug. The spark plugs should be tightened to 20Nm.

AIR FILTER RENEWAL

The MX-5 uses a panel air filter, which is located inside a plastic housing close to the exhaust manifold (the right side of the engine when looking at it from the front of the car). The top section of the plastic housing can be released by undoing a series of metal clips. Once undone, there should be room to remove the old air filter, extract any dirt or debris from inside the housing, then either clean the filter and replace it, or fit a new one.

The standard panel air filter is contained inside a plastic housing and is cheap to renew.

TIMING BELT RENEWAL

The MX-5's timing belt should be renewed every 48,000 miles or four years. At the same time, always renew the

timing belt tensioner and idler pulley. Also, check you have the correct timing belt by looking for a code that indicates the number of teeth on the old belt (for example 145T signifies the belt has 145 teeth) and checking the new belt is the same.

Renewing the timing belt on the MX-5 is reasonably straightforward. There's plenty of space thanks to the front of the engine being at the front of the car. The only trouble with such a layout is that parts of the front of the engine get weather-beaten and corroded, so be patient and sympathetic when undoing many of the exposed fittings. The small 10mm bolts that hold the front timing covers in position usually corrode, so they are prone to shearing off; other components can be equally seized, such as the alternator, power steering pump and their drivebelt tensioners.

Backing off the tensioners for the two auxiliary drivebelts can be difficult if they have seized, so apply lots of penetrating fluid and take a look at the separate section on drivebelts (later in this chapter) for more information, should you get into trouble.

Other difficulties can arise when undoing the 21mm front crankshaft pulley bolt. Space can be a little tight thanks to the front anti-roll bar, so this may need to be dropped down a little by undoing the pair of 12mm bolts for each of its two mounts (*see* the water pump renewal guide later in this chapter for more information and photos). If you find it difficult to undo the large crankshaft bolt with a breaker bar because the engine turns, try using an impact driver instead.

The MX-5's engine is one of a few that has some coolant pipes obstructing the removal of the timing belt. The thermostat is positioned at the front of the engine, just below the camshaft pulleys with coolant pipework leading from it. The only solution is to detach the pipework and lose some coolant. This may be a good opportunity to renew the coolant (*see* the section on Coolant System Flush later in this chapter) and flush out the radiator and engine.

There are a few differences between the Mk1 1600 and 1800 engines and the Mk2 engines when renewing the timing belt, so the following sections give separate instructions for each. For instance, the 1800 has no fan sender unit fitted on top of the thermostat housing. The coil pack is in a different position, but it's still attached to the rocker cover and needs to be moved out of the way.

Timing up the Mazda twin-cam can be confusing. There's a suitable notch and pointer for the crankshaft, but the camshaft pulleys have both E and I markings on each for inlet and exhaust. With the engine timed up, the correct E and I markings should be at 12 o'clock, but the other two markings should face a rib marking on the rear timing belt cover. Some engines have corresponding E and I markings to line these up as well.

If a strut brace is fitted to the engine, it will need to be removed to allow access to the rocker cover. Most strut braces are fitted with long Allen key bolts and captive nuts, which should be easy to remove.

The Mazda twin-cam uses a single timing belt tensioner with a spring and one idler. It's worthwhile renewing the tensioner and idler and inspecting the spring. The spring is attached to a lug on the tensioner and a dowel on the front

of the engine. Use a pair of long-nosed pliers to remove it.

After fitting a new timing belt, tensioner and idler, always manually turn the engine and recheck the timing marks. Also, slacken and retighten the 14mm tensioner bolt to take up any slack in the belt.

TOOLBOX

◆ **Container for draining coolant**
◆ **Screwdrivers**
◆ **Breaker bar (optional)**
◆ **Impact driver**
◆ **Pry bar**
◆ **Sockets/spanners: 10, 12, 14, 21mm**

Time: 90–120 minutes
On your own? Yes

MX-5 Mk1

1. Remove the radiator cap, then raise the vehicle to drain the coolant. There's a drain plug at the front of the car with an access hole through the plastic engine undertray. Some plugs are a bung, which need to be undone with a flat-blade screwdriver.

2. Remove the top radiator hose. Disconnect two breather pipes at the throttle housing, connected to the induction pipe. Undo one 10mm bolt, then remove the induction pipe (some wiring may need unclipping).

3. Disconnect an electrical connection to the power steering pump. Remove the connection to the fan switch on top of the thermostat housing (1600 only). This can break as it's usually brittle. Pinch one side carefully to remove it. Disconnect two pipes from the bottom of the thermostat.

6. Slacken the 12mm pinch bolt for the alternator tensioner, then back off the 12mm adjuster. Push the alternator towards the engine to slacken the drivebelt, then remove with your fingers. Both drivebelts should have now been removed.

4. Slacken the three 10mm bolts on the front of the water pump pulley, followed by the four 10mm bolts on the front crankshaft pulley. These bolts are easier to slacken with the respective drivebelts fitted, so it's better to do so now rather than trying to remove them later when the belts are removed.

7. Remove the three 10mm bolts for the water pump pulley (slackened in step 4) along with the pulley. Undo the four 10mm bolts for the front crankshaft pulley and remove it. Collect the disc washer for the crank pulley.

5. Loosen the 14mm power steering belt tensioner mount bolt. Loosen the 12mm pinch pin, then slacken the 12mm tensioner bolt. Push down on the tensioner and remove the power steering belt with your fingers. Check its condition and renew if worn.

8. Remove the HT leads from the spark plugs. Undo the 12mm bolts that mount the coil pack to the rocker cover, then push the coil pack out of the way. It's still secured by a bolt that's difficult to access, so it can't be fully removed.

9. Undo the eleven 10mm rocker cover bolts (three down the centre and four at each side). Don't undo any of the bolts at the front. Disconnect a breather pipe, then lift the rocker cover off. Remove the top timing belt cover, fitted with four 10mm bolts.

12. Most 1600 and 1800 engines (except some early 1600 engines) have a flange fitted to the crankshaft timing cog. This needs to be removed before the timing belt can be renewed. Undo the 21mm crankshaft pulley bolt, then lever off the flange.

10. Undo one 10mm bolt for the centre timing belt cover and remove the cover. Undo three 10mm bolts for the lower timing belt cover (one on the left and two on the right). Check the seals on all the covers.

13. Slacken the 14mm bolt for the timing belt tensioner. Use a pry bar to adjust and slacken the tensioner, then retighten the bolt. The timing belt should now be slack, so it can be removed with your fingers.

11. Time up the engine by lining a v-notch on the back of the crankshaft timing cog with a pointer at 12 o'clock. The E and I markings on the camshaft pulleys should be lined up with the corresponding letters on the rear timing belt cover.

14. The idler and tensioner can be renewed by undoing their 14mm bolts (disconnect the tensioner spring). The tensioner sits on a pivot dowel. Fit the new timing belt in an anticlockwise direction, starting at the crankshaft cog. Turn the engine manually and recheck the timing marks. Refit all parts and top up the coolant.

MX-5 Mk2

1. After removing the induction pipework, HT leads and the two 12mm bolts that secure the coil pack to the back of the cam cover, remove the camshaft cover, secured with a series of 10mm bolts (plus a few sensors and a breather pipe).

2. There are several sensors to disconnect at the front of the engine before the loom can be moved out of the way and the middle timing belt cover removed. Some fixings are awkward to access, such as this 10mm bolt.

3. The two drivebelts for the alternator/water pump and the power steering pump need to be removed. The water pump pulley has to be removed by undoing three 10mm bolts, which also releases the belt or helps to wind it off.

4. With first gear selected, undo the 21mm bolt on the end of the crankshaft, then remove the front crankshaft pulley. The two lower sections of the timing belt cover can now be removed after undoing a series of 10mm bolts.

5. Refit the 21mm front crankshaft pulley bolt and turn the engine clockwise until the Woodruff key marking is at 12 o'clock and the camshaft timing marks are the same as outlined in step 11 above. You may need to turn the crank another full turn to correctly set the camshaft pulleys.

6. All the hoses need to be detached from the thermostat housing to change the timing belt, so it's also worthwhile renewing the coolant. In this case, unscrew a plastic plug from the bottom of the radiator to drain the coolant into a container.

7. The old timing belt can now be removed. First, adjust the tensioner by slackening its centre bolt, adjusting it with a pry bar and tightening the bolt again to slacken the belt. The old belt can then be removed by hand.

8. Renew the timing belt tensioner and idler pulley, refitting their original bolts with thread lock and positioning the tensioner so the belt will be slack, making it easier to fit. There's a new retaining spring to fit, which is a little awkward.

9. Fit the new timing belt, adjust the tensioner, then manually turn the engine on the crankshaft pulley bolt two full turns before rechecking the timing marks. Refit all remaining parts and refill or top up the coolant.

RADIATOR RENEWAL

The MX-5's radiator is mounted at the front of the engine bay and has to be one of the easiest to remove, with only a few fittings to undo and lots of space around it. It's therefore worth removing the radiator to inspect and flush it out every four or five years. If you need to renew it, a new radiator isn't very expensive.

Before you start removing the radiator, make sure the engine and its coolant are cold. Do not release the radiator's pressure cap if the engine is hot because you may get scalded by the hot coolant that's stored under pressure.

When draining the old coolant, dispose of it at your local council depot – do not pour it down the drain. Engine coolant is extremely poisonous if swallowed by humans or animals, so dispose of it properly.

After fitting a new radiator and topping up the coolant, check the coolant level in the expansion bottle every day for a few days to ensure there is no fluid loss. You may find that some of the coolant hoses have been disturbed and are leaking. Also, old hose clips can weaken, so they may also need to be renewed.

TOOLBOX

◆ *Antifreeze*
◆ *Bottle brush*
◆ *Drain bowl*
◆ *Hosepipe*
◆ *Penetrating fluid*
◆ *Screwdrivers*
◆ *Sockets/spanners: 7–14mm*
◆ *Trim tool*
◆ *Vice grips*

Time: 30 minutes
On your own? Yes

1. Drain the coolant from the radiator. There should be a plastic crosshead drain plug in the middle of the bottom of the radiator. If the engine is warm or hot, the coolant may scald you, so wait until it has completely cooled down.

2. If a front undertray is fitted, it's worth removing it so you can access the hose that's connected to the bottom of the radiator. The undertray is usually secured with 10mm bolts and screws, many of which can shear off.

5. Try to detach the top hose from the radiator. After releasing the spring clip, you may find it difficult to part the hose from the radiator. Detaching it from the thermostat housing is usually easier.

3. Detach the hose that's connected to the bottom of the radiator (right side when looking from the front of the car). A spring clip should be fitted here, so pull the exposed ends together with vice grips to slacken and move the clip.

6. If the top of the radiator is secured at each corner with a small metal plate, these will need to be removed. They are usually retained with one 14mm nut. Apply penetrating fluid if they seem to be seized.

4. From within the engine bay, remove the induction pipe that's routed across the radiator to make more space. It's secured at each end with a jubilee clip that can be undone with a screwdriver or 7–10mm socket.

7. Detach the small rubber pipe that's connected between the top of the radiator (in the centre) and the plastic expansion bottle. To avoid coolant leaking everywhere, only detach it from the radiator.

8. Detach the electrical plug for the cooling fan. You should now be ready to remove the radiator. It sits in locating points at the bottom corners, so try to lift it up and out of the engine bay.

11. Inspect the condition of the cooling fins, especially at the front of the radiator. If the fins are crumbling away, like the ones shown here, the radiator should be renewed.

9. If you would like to reuse your radiator, try flushing it through using a hosepipe. This will also help to assess whether the radiator is blocked or contains lots of debris.

12. If you are renewing the radiator, swap over the cooling fan to the new one. Undo the four 10mm bolts that secure the fan to the back of the radiator. These bolts will probably be corroded, so spray over them with penetrating fluid.

10. Manually rotate the electric cooling fan to ensure it spins freely and there is no noise from the bearings. If the fan feels stiff to rotate or it wobbles, it may be a good idea to replace it.

13. The four 10mm bolts that secure the electric fan to the radiator are threaded into square nuts, which are housed in plastic on the radiator. The plastic usually breaks and the nuts spin, so grip them with vice grips. The bolts often shear.

14. After transferring the electric fan and securing it with new bolts if the old ones are corroded or have sheared, manually rotate the fan to make sure it doesn't foul the radiator and that it spins freely.

15. It's worth removing the coolant expansion bottle from the engine bay to clean it out. It's secured to the inner wing with a couple of nuts and bolts. These can shear off, so spray penetrating fluid over them.

16. With the coolant expansion bottle removed, clean it out with a bottle brush and pour lots of water into it. If the bottle is full of dirt, you may not be able to judge the coolant level for the engine.

17. When you're ready to fit the new radiator or refit the old one, lower it into the engine bay, then reconnect the lower hose, followed by the top hose and small pipe from the expansion bottle. Attach the plug for the fan, the top mounts and refit the induction pipe.

18. Pour an appropriate mixture of antifreeze and water (or pre-mixed) into the top of the radiator until it's full. The pink-coloured coolant shown here has a five-year lifespan, whereas blue coolant has two years.

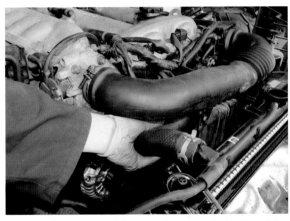

19. Run the engine with the radiator cap left off and the heater set to maximum hot. Eventually the thermostat will open and warm coolant will flow through the top hose and into the radiator. Top up the coolant if required.

20. Refit the radiator cap (renew it if you are unsure of its age) and leave the engine running until the electric fan is activated. Switch off the engine, check for leaks and check the level in the expansion bottle after the engine has cooled down.

Coolant System Flush

The MX-5's coolant system is very straightforward to maintain, so there's no excuse not to renew the coolant at the recommended service intervals (every two or five years, depending on the type of coolant used) and flush the engine and radiator through to remove any debris.

The radiator can be removed in less than half an hour, so it's worth taking it out of the engine bay to inspect it and attach a hosepipe to it to help flush it through (*see* above).

The plastic coolant expansion tank that's fitted to the

The radiator is quite straightforward to remove and easier to inspect and flush through when it's out of the engine bay.

inner wing (driver's side of RHD cars) should be removed to clean it out. Dirt can build up inside it, resulting in the outlet to the radiator becoming blocked. This can have catastrophic results if the coolant in the expansion tank cannot be fed through to the radiator. If the coolant in the engine and radiator runs low, the expansion bottle may remain full, so you are fooled into thinking there's no problem with the engine coolant.

DRIVEBELT RENEWAL

There are two drivebelts on the MX-5 engine, which are driven off the crankshaft and are connected to the alternator, water pump and power steering pump (air conditioning pump as well on some models). With all of these components being fitted at the front of the engine, they are easy to access, but can quickly corrode due to the amount of road dirt they are exposed to. Consequently, the alternator and power steering pump often become difficult to move and thus difficult to adjust the tension on their drivebelts. The alternator can be particularly difficult because its lower mounting bolt (pinch bolt) has to be slackened to adjust the tension on its drivebelt, and space is tight, especially on engines where the head of the bolt cannot be seen.

TOOLBOX

◆ **Penetrating fluid**
◆ **Pry bar**
◆ **Sockets/spanners: 10–21mm**

Time: 30 minutes
On your own? Yes

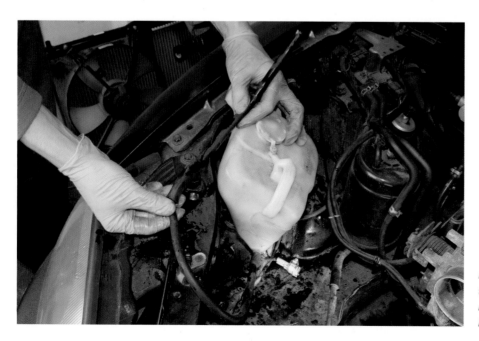

Remove the coolant expansion tank and clean inside it to remove any dirt that could block its pipe to the radiator.

The best advice is to keep on top of maintenance of the drivebelts. Check the respective tensioners and undo all the mounting bolts on a regular basis (at least once a year), and keep them lubricated with a little light grease.

The following steps outline what's involved in renewing both drivebelts on an engine without air conditioning.

1. Remove the induction pipework across the front of the engine to help provide better access to the water pump. This is secured with jubilee clips or similar clips with 7–10mm fastenings.

2. Slacken the 14mm nut and bolt that prevents the power steering pump from moving. This can be seen through the holes in the power steering pump pulley. Make sure the nut at the back doesn't spin at the same time.

3. Slacken the locking nut for the power steering drivebelt adjuster, as shown here, then wind out the long bolt next to it to help slacken the belt. Push down on the power steering pump to help move it.

4. Once the power steering pump drivebelt is sufficiently slack, it should be possible to remove it with your fingers. If this isn't possible, try winding it off by turning the crankshaft pulley via its 21mm centre bolt.

5. Undo the 12mm or 14mm pinch bolt that secures the bottom of the alternator and prevents it moving. The head of the bolt may be difficult to access and undo. Apply lots of penetrating fluid to help release it.

6. Undo the locking bolt on the top of the alternator, then wind out the adjuster bolt shown here to help slacken the alternator drivebelt. Hopefully the drivebelt will start to become slack and can be removed by hand.

7. If the alternator belt cannot be removed because it's not slack, but all of the bolts mentioned in the previous steps have been slackened, try levering against the alternator to move it and slacken the belt.

10. After fitting the new drivebelts and adjusting their tensioners (each belt should be tight enough to be able to twist it a quarter of a turn), run the engine. Check the tension of the belts and adjust again after a test drive.

WATER PUMP RENEWAL

The water pump is located at the front of the engine and driven by the alternator drivebelt. It can fail if the drivebelt is too tight, but also fail due to general wear and tear. Remove the drivebelt and spin the pulley to check it rotates freely, then waggle the pulley up and down to check for play in the bearings.

Renewing the water pump is quite time-consuming, so it's a good idea to carry out a few additional jobs at the same time, such as changing the auxiliary drivebelts and timing belt and refreshing the engine coolant. The water pump is concealed by the camshaft pulleys, so these need to be removed. Consequently the timing belt has to be removed. All the coolant inside the engine will escape, so it's best to renew this as well.

8. Check the new drivebelt is the same as the old one: look for codes on the exterior or compare their lengths. Also make sure the new drivebelt has the same number of ribs as the old one.

9. Fit each new drivebelt by hand. If the power steering pump or alternator proved to be difficult to move, you may have to resort to winding the new belt on via the 21mm crankshaft pulley bolt.

TOOLBOX

- ◆ *Drain bowl*
- ◆ *Multi-purpose grease*
- ◆ *Open-ended spanner (23–24mm)*
- ◆ *Penetrating fluid*
- ◆ *Pry bar*
- ◆ *Rubber mallet*
- ◆ *Sockets/spanners: 10–21mm*
- ◆ *Torque wrench*

Time: 3–4 hours
On your own? Yes

1. Remove the induction pipework from across the front of the engine and detach the coolant top hose. With the drivebelts fitted, slacken the three 10mm bolts that secure the pulley to the front of the water pump. This is easier than doing it after the belt has been removed.

4. Detach the HT leads from the spark plugs. Remove the camshaft cover, which is secured with a series of bolts (including those at the rear for the coil pack). Undo the 10mm bolts that secure the front timing belt covers and remove them.

2. Remove the drivebelts (*see* above), then fully undo the 10mm bolts for the water pump pulley and remove it. The pulley may need a few taps with a rubber mallet to release it.

5. Remove the crankshaft pulley (*see* the timing belt section above for further details), then time up the engine to make sure the markings on the camshafts line up with those on the adjacent rear timing cover. There's also a timing notch on the crankshaft.

3. The wiring loom that is routed across the front of the engine needs to be moved out of the way to allow the front timing belt covers and the camshaft cover to be removed. Detach this wiring and any mounting brackets.

6. Slacken the camshaft pulley bolts, but do not fully undo them. The camshaft pulleys (sprockets) need to be removed in order to remove the water pump. Check the timing marks are still correct.

7. Slacken the timing belt tensioner's centre bolt, adjust it so that the belt becomes slack, then tighten it again. The timing belt can now be removed and should ideally be renewed along with the tensioner and idler.

10. The rear timing belt cover can now be removed. This has to be removed to access the water pump. It's secured with six bolts.

8. Remove the timing belt tensioner and idler pulley. These are secured to the water pump and need to be removed to make it easier to remove the water pump later. Both are secured with a single 14mm bolt.

11. Detach any pipes or electrical plugs connected to the thermostat housing, then undo its two mounting bolts and remove. These mounting bolts may be awkward to access, with space for a spanner only.

9. Check the camshaft pulleys are in the correct position, then undo each mounting bolt and remove. Note how each pulley is fitted on the locating dowel on the end of the camshaft. Store safely aside.

12. The water pump is almost ready to be removed. Look at the right side of it and undo two 12mm bolts that secure an outlet pipe to it. These are awkward to access, but must be undone.

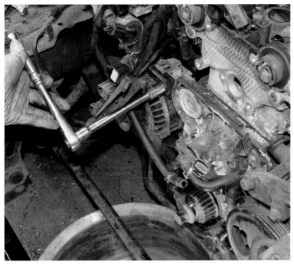

13. The alternator has a mounting bracket attached to the left side of the water pump. Undo the bolt that's fitted through the bracket and into the body of the water pump.

16. Here are all of the parts that have been removed to allow the water pump to be renewed. Replace any bolts that are heavily corroded and check the condition of the camshaft cover seal.

14. The water pump can now be removed, so undo its four 12mm bolts and have a container ready underneath to catch any coolant that escapes from the engine.

17. Clean the mating face of the engine where the water pump is fitted. Traces of the old gasket may need to be removed. Also clean the mating surface of the outlet pipe that's connected to the side of the water pump.

15. The water pump may need a gentle tap around the edges with a rubber mallet, or a little leverage to help release it. If it refuses to move check you have undone all of its fittings.

18. Before fitting the new water pump check the new gaskets are the correct size and make sure all of the mounting bolts can be fitted. Also check that the new water pump is the same as the old one.

19. Carefully fit the new water pump into position. Some people prefer to add a smear of grease between the gasket and the engine to ensure it can be removed and reused in the future. Tighten all of the mounting bolts to 20Nm.

21. Fit a new timing belt tensioner and idler (tighten to 50Nm) followed by a new timing belt, checking the timing marks are correctly aligned. Adjust the tension on the belt, then turn the engine manually via the crankshaft pulley bolt and recheck the timing marks.

20. Refit all the remaining bolts for the water pump, then refit the camshaft pulleys. Use a large open-ended spanner (24mm) to secure the camshaft (look for a suitable flat) and tighten the camshaft pulley bolts to 60Nm.

22. If the camshafts are under load when fitting the timing belt, you may need to hold them with open-ended spanners to maintain their correct timing and fit the belt at the same time. This usually requires help from someone else.

23. When you've finished refitting all remaining parts, refill the coolant and run the engine with the heater on maximum hot and the radiator pressure cap removed to extract any air before refitting the cap. Check the level when the engine is cold.

FUEL PUMP TROUBLE

The fuel tank on the MX-5 is located between the boot and the interior. The fuel pump is fitted inside the tank and a common problem that can arise on the Mk2 concerns fuel starvation. This arises when the fuel level is low and the car is cornering, usually when it's cornering left. If the end of the fuel pump's pickup pipe is damaged, it will struggle to draw fuel, especially when the fuel level is low and the petrol is sloshing around inside the tank under cornering. The resulting symptoms are a loss of engine power for a few seconds. The engine probably won't stall (unless the fuel level is very low) – it just loses power a little, then regains it once the fuel settles inside the petrol tank.

The answer to this problem is to remove the fuel pump and inspect the bottom of the pickup, where there is a piece of gauze. If the fuel pump has been removed before, the gauze end can easily get damaged upon refitting. It can catch the sides of the petrol tank, causing the gauze to become folded over, which restricts its ability to draw in fuel. In some cases, the gauze can be straightened out and the fuel pump refitted with care to avoid damaging the end again.

Accessing the fuel pump is reasonably time-consuming. The parcel shelf carpet needs to be removed and, ideally, the back of the hood needs to be detached and pulled forwards. This requires a series of 10mm nuts to be undone and three lengths of metal removed to release the back of the hood from the bodywork. This creates more space than folding the hood down – and don't try to remove the fuel pump from inside the MX-5 with the hood up as you may be overcome with petrol fumes.

Take extra care when extracting the fuel pump. Have a few cloths or paper towels ready to catch any petrol that spills out. Work in a ventilated area and wear gloves to avoid contaminating your skin.

TOOLBOX

- **Cloths or paper towels**
- **Gloves**
- **Sockets/spanners: 10, 12, 14mm**
- **Screwdrivers**

Time: 90 minutes
On your own? Yes

1. The fuel pump is secured to the top of the petrol tank, which can be accessed via the rear parcel shelf. First, the back of the hood needs to be detached and pulled forward to create more space. A metal plate covers the pump and tank, secured with crosshead screws.

4. Carefully lift the fuel pump out from the tank. Look for signs of damage, such as the gauze and pickup at the bottom of the pump being folded over. This sort of damage can sometimes be repaired by straightening the parts out.

2. The top of the fuel pump is secured to the fuel tank with a series of small screws that can easily drop down and never be seen again, so carefully remove them and check you have some spares, just in case.

5. Thoroughly clean the fuel pump's pickup, then straighten it and check it will remain straight. Due to the shape of the petrol tank, it's easy to bend the end of the pickup. Refit the pump to see if the problem has been fixed.

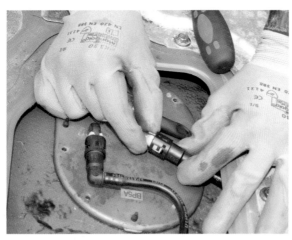

3. Detach the plug connector and the two fuel pipe connections, making sure the white plastic innards are retained. These have to be carefully eased off the ends of the pipes on the fuel pump and refitted to the ends of the fuel pipes.

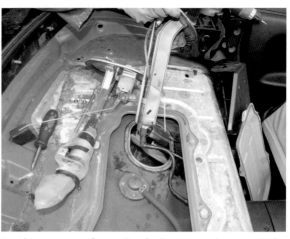

6. If you want to fit another fuel pump, make sure it's the correct type and from the same era of MX-5. The photograph here shows a fuel pump from a Mk1 MX-5, which cannot be fitted into the fuel tank of a Mk2.

engine tuning

PERFORMANCE AIR FILTERS

A relatively cheap starting point for modifying the MX-5's engine and gaining a few extra bhp is to change the standard air filter for a performance product. The MX-5 uses a closed induction system with a panel filter concealed in a plastic box and a feed pipe that takes air from around the nearside front of the engine bay. The air is then drawn through a pipe that is fitted across the front of the engine to a single throttle body on the offside of the engine bay. A mass airflow meter is fitted close to the air filter box and on the Mk2 there's also an air temperature sensor.

One of the cheapest air filter upgrades is to fit a performance panel filter, which will usually produce an extra 1–2bhp. If you want a more noticeable power gain then an open cone is the next step, but sometimes these can reduce performance, especially if they are restrictive or positioned in the engine bay so that all they draw in is warm air. Cold-

A performance panel filter is a popular starting point for engine modifications and usually produces an additional 1–2bhp.

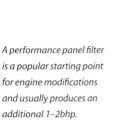

air feeds can often help with an open cone, which directs air from outside over the top of it. Better results can often be achieved by fitting a closed induction system, which consists of a cone inside a box with a cold-air feed. This is sometimes too restrictive, however, especially on turbo- or supercharged engines with a high power output.

TOOLBOX

♦ **Ratchet and long extension bars**
♦ **Screwdrivers**
♦ **Spanners/sockets: 10, 12, 14mm**

Time: 45 minutes
On your own? Yes

Fitting a K&N 57i Open Cone

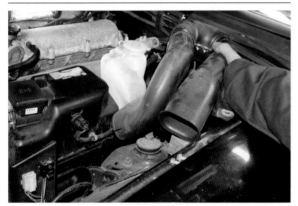

1. Remove the induction pipework that feeds air into the standard air box. This is secured to the nearside inner wing with a couple of 10mm bolts. The pipework slots into the air box, so it should be straightforward to remove.

2. The MX-5's standard air box needs to be removed. In the case of the Mk2, an air temperature sensor is fitted to the side of the air box, so this needs to be pulled out and will be fitted later into the cone.

3. The MX-5's MAF meter is also retained, but needs to be removed. First of all, disconnect its electrical plug. Pinch the tab on the side of the plug to release it, then carefully slide it off.

4. Undo the clip that secures the induction hose on to the MAF meter. This may be a large jubilee clip, or as shown here, a clip with a 10mm nut and bolt – the nut is supposed to remain secure, but not in this case.

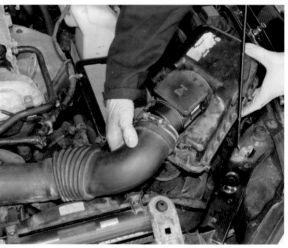

5. Release the metal clips that secure the air filter box's lid in position. Remove the lid and detach the induction hose from the MAF meter. The lid can now be removed from the engine bay, but don't discard it as the MAF meter is required.

6. Undo the two 10mm bolts that secure the MAF meter to the lid of the air filter box. Carefully remove the MAF meter along with the rubber seal, which will probably fall off. Don't discard the two 10mm bolts as they will be needed later.

9. Fit a large jubilee clip (supplied in the 57i kit) around the base of the new open cone air filter. Next, fit the end of the MAF meter (the end that was fitted into the standard air box) into the open cone.

7. The K&N 57i open cone can sit inside the base of the standard air filter box, but it's best to remove it and create more space. It's secured with a couple of bolts that require a socket and long extension bar to undo. Once undone, lift the base of the air filter box out of the engine bay.

10. Carefully feed the air temperature sensor that was removed in step 2 (this shouldn't apply to the Mk1 MX-5) into the hole in the base of the 57i open cone air filter. This will be a reasonably tight fit and there is no other means of keeping it secure.

8. An angled bracket is supplied in the 57i kit and has to be secured to a mounting bracket near the power steering pump. It will be attached to the side of the MAF meter later. First, undo the 12mm bolt above the power steering pump pulley, then refit it with the bracket shown here.

11. Refit the MAF meter's electrical plug that was removed in step 3, then fit the air filter and MAF meter back on to the induction pipe. Make sure the wiring for the MAF meter and air temperature sensor are not stretched.

12. Refit one of the 10mm bolts for the MAF meter (*see* step 6) through the top hole in the angled bracket that was fitted in step 8 and into the side of the MAF meter. This helps to keep it steady. Tighten all jubilee clips.

EXHAUST UPGRADES

There are a number of performance exhaust manifolds and systems for the MX-5, which help to improve the breathability of the engine and complement other upgrades. Problems, however, can soon arise when you attempt to remove an old exhaust system. The heat from the exhaust corrodes most of the fittings, so be prepared for sheared studs and bolts. Penetrating fluid and a blowtorch are essential.

One of the easiest exhaust-related upgrades is to change the rear silencer. This is perhaps the most straightforward on an amateur DIY level, especially if you don't have access to a pit or a ramp. On the Mk2 MX-5 there should be two nuts that secure the silencer to the rest of the exhaust system. These may be heavily corroded, so spray over them with penetrating fluid and find a suitable socket that grips them sufficiently (around 15mm). Once undone, lever off the silencer's rubber hangers so the heavy silencer can be removed – use axle stands to support it and prevent it from dropping on to you. When it comes to fitting another silencer, raise it into position with trolley jacks and axle stands.

The standard silencer at the rear of the Mk2 MX-5 is quite heavy.

The exhaust system forward of the rear silencer includes a mid-pipe, mid-silencer and catalytic converter. This may be joined in the centre, making it easier to remove in parts. Sadly, this doesn't apply in all cases, especially if the system has been repaired, so you may find the exhaust system is one piece from the mid-section to the rear silencer – this makes it difficult to remove without a ramp or pit.

On the Mk2 MX-5 there should be a couple of nuts that secure the rear silencer to the rest of the system.

This Mk1 MX-5's standard exhaust system doesn't appear to have any separations, which makes it awkward to remove without a ramp or pit.

Further problems can emerge when you start trying to undo fittings underneath the car. The two nuts that secure the front of the catalytic converter to the end of the down-pipe are usually heavily corroded and often require an impact driver to undo them, along with penetrating fluid and heat from a blowtorch. Fortunately, these are easy to access if the car is over a pit or raised on a ramp.

Two rusty nuts usually secure the catalytic converter to the end of the downpipe.

The hardest fittings to undo are where the downpipe is connected to the end of the exhaust manifold. These are squeezed between the gearbox and front subframe, so space is tight. If any problems arise, the exhaust manifold will usually need to be removed to fix them.

The fittings where the exhaust manifold is attached to the system are difficult to access and often seized.

Finally, if you want to change the exhaust manifold, this involves undoing the aforementioned fittings from underneath where the end of the manifold is connected to the exhaust system. From within the engine bay, the heatshield has to be removed to access the 14mm manifold nuts. These are usually corroded, so apply lots of penetrating fluid first.

The exhaust manifold nuts are usually corroded, so apply penetrating fluid to help undo them.

THROTTLE BODY CONVERSION

The multi-point fuel injection system on the MX-5 with its single throttle body and plenum is frugal, efficient and quiet. When it comes to modifications and more performance, once you've fitted a performance air filter, the next stage in the quest for more power is a big leap in the direction of throttle bodies and engine management.

Individual throttle bodies are more efficient at allowing equal amounts of air into all of the four cylinders on the MX-5 twin-cam engine. A standard set-up uses only one throttle body to feed the air into a plenum chamber, and as Mike Longstaff at Roadrunner Racing explains: 'The early MX-5 had a very restrictive vane type mass air flow sensor; the later type uses a hot wire mass air flow sensor, which is an improvement, but still very restrictive.'

The following step-by-step guide reveals what's involved in removing the standard fuel injection system from the MX-5's engine and fitting a set of Jenvey throttle bodies. This isn't a straightforward conversion. For instance, a programmable ECU is required to ensure the throttle bodies can operate correctly. It also needs the correct type of air filter to get the most from the throttle bodies and avoid strangling them. There are plenty of minor details that need careful consideration, such as the fitting of sensors, the removal of standard injectors and the amount of engine bay space available, which sometimes restricts the fitting of particular parts (for example an air filter and fuel rail).

TOOLBOX

♦ **Cloths**
♦ **Drill and drill bits**
♦ **Hammer**
♦ **Screwdrivers**
♦ **Spanners/sockets: 10, 12, 14mm**

Time: 1–2 days
On your own? Yes

Removing the Old Fuel Injection System

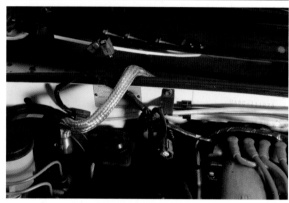

1. Detach the vacuum hose between the brake servo and the inlet manifold along with any electrical connectors (label them). The servo pipe will be refitted to the new inlet manifold to ensure the brakes remain servo-assisted.

2. Disconnect the fuel lines to the fuel rail and any electrical connections, then remove the fuel rail and injectors. Wipe up any spilled fuel and block or drain any pipes that leak fuel.

3. Remove the induction system fitted onto the standard throttle body. For further details, *see* the previous section on fitting a K&N 57i, which explains how to remove these parts.

4. Disconnect the electrical plugs, pipework and accelerator cable that are attached to the throttle body. Label all connections, as these will be required when fitting the new throttle bodies.

5. Detach any pipes and other connections from the plenum and inlet manifold, then remove this assembly by undoing the nuts that secure it to the side of the cylinder head. The injectors need to be removed from the cylinder head on the 1800 engine.

6. A coolant pipe on the top of the oil filter housing feeds coolant to the throttle body (acting as a water-heated inlet manifold). This won't be used with the throttle bodies, so join it to the return pipe.

Fitting the Throttle Bodies

1. Blanks need to be fitted into the injector holes on the 1800 cylinder head – store these in a freezer for 24 hours to make them easier to fit. Also fit a new inlet manifold gasket on to the side of the cylinder head.

2. A new adjustable fuel pressure regulator may need to be fitted (the old one is part of the original fuel rail) and the fuel lines connected to it. In some cases, this can be mounted close to the brake master cylinder and brake fluid reservoir.

3. The throttle bodies can be assembled on a bench, securing them to the inlet manifold, fitting the fuel rail and original injectors and loosely fitting the trumpets. A vacuum servo outlet needs to be drilled and tapped.

4. The throttle body assembly can now be lowered into position and secured to the cylinder head with new nuts. Progressively tighten all the mounting nuts using spanners and sockets.

5. Fit the brake servo vacuum hose onto the appropriate outlet on the new inlet manifold. Connect the accelerator cable to the throttle linkage on the new throttle bodies.

6. If any of the trumpets had to be removed to make room for fitting the throttle bodies, they can be re-fitted now and secured with their clamps and bolts. They may need to be removed again later when fitting an air filter.

7. The original wiring for the injectors can be refitted. A new air temperature sensor will need to be fitted elsewhere in the engine bay (not near the exhaust) and a new connector made for the throttle position sensor on the throttle bodies.

8. There are a couple of breather pipes attached to the camshaft cover. These can be vented to the atmosphere via a small filter, or routed to a catch tank to collect the vapours from the top of the engine.

Space can often dictate what size of filter, if any, can be fitted on to throttle bodies. Some form of filtration is essential to help reduce the risk of drawing debris into the engine and causing damage. If space is very tight, then mesh may be the only answer, but this may restrict airflow. Similarly a foam air filter can also restrict airflow if it's positioned too close to the ends of the throttle bodies.

SUPERCHARGER CONVERSION

The MX-5's range of twin-cam engines seems to be strong enough to withstand the forced induction of supercharging, and various conversion kits are readily available.

In brief, a supercharger is a mechanical pump that can be used to force air into an engine, instead of using the

engine to draw it in. In the case of a car engine, it's belt-driven via the crankshaft, just like an alternator or power steering pump. Air gets drawn into the supercharger and forced out. This forced air is fed into the engine, but first it can travel through an intercooler to reduce its temperature and increase the density of oxygen.

The larger quantity of air generated by the supercharger needs to be matched with a larger quantity of fuel, so the fuel system needs to be uprated with larger injectors (360–440cc with high impedance for the MX-5). The yellow injectors from the Mazda RX-8 for instance, can be used on the MX-5 engine.

The MX-5's standard ECU cannot be used with a supercharger conversion as it needs to be re-programmed to cope with the changes in fuelling and induction. There are a number of different programmable ECUs available. The following photographs show the Megasquirt MS2 programmable ECU. They also show how to fit a supercharger from a BMW Mini Cooper S (2000–2006) to a Mk1 or Mk2 Mazda MX-5. You'll also need a bypass valve from a Cooper S and a throttle body from a 1.6 MX-5. If the conversion is being fitted onto a 1.8-litre engine, some throttle linkage modifications are required to the car's original throttle body, which are outlined in detail over the following pages.

Various conversion kits are available to allow a range of superchargers to be fitted to the MX-5 engine. The photographs over the next few pages show such a kit from Ewens Sports Cars in the UK being fitted.

The work involved for this conversion starts with some engine bay preparation. The standard air filter housing and its feed pipe need to be removed. The feed pipe is secured to the side of the inner wing with 10mm bolts. The air filter housing's lid needs to be released and removed, along with the MAF sensor, by undoing a jubilee or hose clip and disconnecting any electrical plugs. The MAF sensor isn't required any more with this particular conversion, but the air temperature sensor, which is fitted into the side of the air filter housing on the Mk2, must be refitted into the induction pipework close to the car's throttle body.

If an intercooler is being fitted to the car the standard induction pipe that's routed across the front of the engine can be removed. This is secured with jubilee clips and some bolts underneath the resonator box. If an intercooler is not being fitted then this pipework can be reused if required.

The supercharger is secured to the exhaust manifold side of the engine, so the standard heatshield has to be removed and discarded. The front mounting lug for this heatshield needs to be cut or ground off to allow the supercharger's mounting bracket to be fitted. This mounting lug is part of the exhaust manifold.

The supercharger is powered by the drivebelt that also drives the power steering pump. The standard tensioner assembly for this drivebelt needs to be replaced with a new assembly and a longer belt.

A mounting bracket for the supercharger is secured to one of the exhaust manifold studs and engine lifting eyes. The supercharger is bolted to this bracket and also to the new drivebelt tensioner assembly.

Before the supercharger is fitted, it needs to be assembled with a new inlet and outlet manifold, a bypass valve and a 1.6 throttle body.

Once the supercharger has been fitted, an air filter can be fitted on to its throttle body and its pipework routed to the car's original throttle body (via an intercooler if desired).

This supercharger conversion kit is manufactured by Ewens Sports Cars of Peterborough.

The Eaton supercharger from the BMW Mini Cooper S can be fitted onto the MX-5 engine.

In theory, this supercharger conversion should take less than half a day to complete, but only if you are lucky and everything goes smoothly. In reality, set aside a long weekend to complete the conversion, allowing time to fabricate mounting brackets for an intercooler, experiment with pipework and resolve unforeseen problems.

HOW OLD IS SUPERCHARGING?

Supercharging was invented before the motor car. Brothers Francis and Philander Roots had designed a bi-rotor gear pump for their watermill, but it wasn't particularly good. Luckily, they discovered it was better at pumping large amounts of air into a foundry furnace, so they patented its design in 1860 and continued to develop it, filing a further sixteen patents by 1884. Their design of a supercharger has been used on everything from motor car engines to trucks and trains.

TOOLBOX

◆ *Allen keys: 4, 6, 8mm*
◆ *Angle grinder, gloves and safety goggles*
◆ *Drainage tray*
◆ *MIG welder (1.8 engine only)*
◆ *Penetrating fluid*
◆ *Petroleum jelly*
◆ *Pillar drill and 3mm drill bit (1.8 engine only)*
◆ *Screwdrivers*
◆ *Sealant*
◆ *Sockets/spanners: 10, 12, 14, 17mm*

Time required: Weekend
On your own: Yes

Engine Bay Preparation

1. Remove the standard air filter housing along with the MAF sensor. The induction pipe that runs across the front of the engine to the throttle body can be reused if an intercooler isn't going to be fitted. Otherwise it should be removed.

4. Remove the exhaust manifold heatshield, secured with 10mm bolts. The supercharger is secured to the exhaust manifold and cylinder head, so the heatshield has to be removed. Also remove the engine lifting eye attached to the cylinder head (14mm bolt).

2. If an intercooler is going to be fitted, drain and remove the radiator. There's a drain plug on the base, but remove the engine undertray to access the bottom hose. The radiator is secured with two 12mm or 14mm nuts at the top corners.

5. Grind or cut off the heatshield's front mounting lug on the exhaust manifold. This has to be removed to allow a mounting bracket to be fitted for the supercharger – *see* step 7 for details on fitting the mounting bracket.

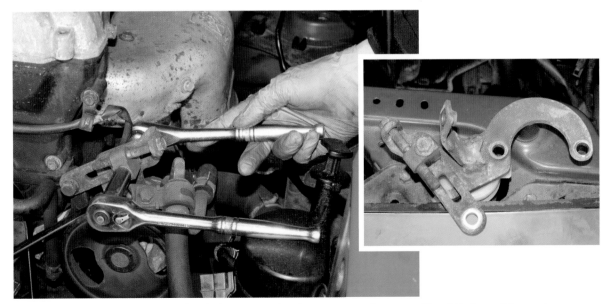

3. The supercharger will be driven by a belt connected to the power steering pump. The old belt won't be used, so remove it along with its adjuster assembly. Undo a series of 12mm and 14mm bolts to release the belt and remove the assembly.

6. Apply penetrating fluid to the exhaust manifold stud shown here (second upper from the front), then undo its 14mm nut. The supercharger's mounting bracket will be fitted over this stud in the next step.

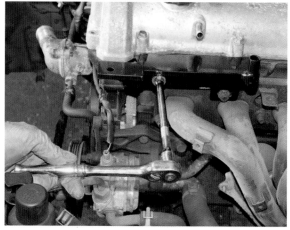

7. Fit the mounting bracket for the supercharger, securing it to the exhaust manifold via the stud whose nut was undone in the last step, and the 14mm bolt for the engine lifting eye. Check the mounting bracket doesn't foul the mounting lug that was ground off in step 5.

8. Fit the new drivebelt tensioner assembly supplied in the kit from Ewens Sports Cars. This is secured to the original points on the engine where the old assembly was located. There are also a couple of pulleys that need to be fitted (tensioner and idler).

Assembling the Supercharger

1. Fit a blanking plate on the end of the Mini Cooper S supercharger and secure it with four 10mm bolts. This plate is supplied in the kit from Ewens Sports Cars and covers the rotating parts of the supercharger, ensuring fingers and debris don't get trapped inside.

2. Fit the outlet manifold with a new gasket onto the supercharger and secure with four 6mm Allen key bolts (fit flat and spring washers with each bolt). These parts are included in the supercharger conversion kit.

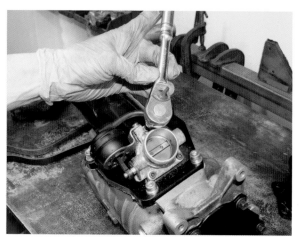

3. Take a Mini Cooper S bypass valve and its three 4mm Allen key bolts and fit it on top of the outlet manifold. The bypass valve controls the flow of air from the supercharger, especially at idle. It has its own rubber seal, so it doesn't need a gasket.

4. A new inlet manifold is included in the kit and should be secured onto the end of the supercharger with sealant, leaving it to dry for at least 24 hours before running the engine. The MX-5 1.6 throttle body will be attached to this, along with an air filter.

6. Undo the 12mm nut on the end of the 1.6 throttle body and remove the linkage (1.8 engines only). Use a pillar drill and 3mm drill bit to drill through the two dowels that secure the short throttle cable guide to the linkage, as shown here. Reassemble the linkage.

5. Undo three crosshead screws for the air control valve on the MX-5 1.6 throttle body, remove it and fit a blanking plate from the kit and secure it with the same screws. The throttle position sensor (TPS) also needs to be removed, which is secured with two 6mm screws.

7. Fit the 1.6 throttle body on to the inlet manifold of the supercharger with a new gasket, nuts and bolts and two angled brackets between it and the supercharger (all parts are supplied in the kit).

8. Fit a short length of stainless steel pipe with silicone hoses at each end (supplied in the kit) between the outlet on the new inlet manifold and the Mini Cooper S bypass valve fitted on the outlet manifold. Secure them with jubilee clips.

Fitting the Supercharger

1. After assembling the supercharger with its inlet and outlet manifolds, bypass valve, modified MX-5 1.6 throttle body and external pipework, manoeuvre everything into position over the exhaust manifold to see how it should be fitted.

2. Secure the supercharger assembly to the new mounting bracket with two nuts and bolts (supplied in the kit). Fit another bolt through the new drivebelt tensioner assembly and into the supercharger. Progressively tighten all of these bolts.

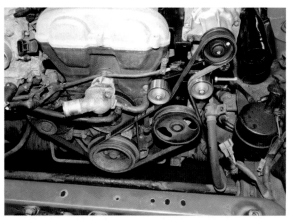

3. Fit a new longer drivebelt (supplied in the kit) and adjust the tensioner until it is tight. Make sure the idler and tensioner pulleys' mounting bolts are fully tightened. The drivebelt will need to be checked and its tensioner adjusted again after running the engine.

4. On 1.8 engines, tack weld the small throttle cable guide to the linkage on the car's throttle body (disconnect the battery). This was removed in step 6 of the previous section and will be used to fit a second throttle cable to the second throttle body.

5. Fit a short bicycle brake cable and sleeving to connect the car's original throttle body linkage to the second throttle body on the supercharger. The accelerator cable's mounting bracket on the plenum chamber will need to be modified to accommodate the second cable.

6. Fit an air filter on to the end of the second throttle body. Space is tight here, and more so if the car has ABS. There is usually room to fit a silicone hose elbow, followed by an open cone air filter.

Miscellaneous Supercharger Items

1. If an intercooler is being fitted, reposition the electric fan on the radiator to the centre using new mounting brackets supplied in the kit from Ewens Sports Cars. The radiator will be refitted after fitting the intercooler in the next step.

2. An intercooler can be fitted inside the front bumper using home-made mounting brackets. Pipework has to be made and fitted between it and the car's throttle body and also to the supercharger.

3. The injectors need to be uprated to 360–440cc with high impedance (for example yellow Mazda RX-8 ones). Undo three 12mm bolts for the fuel rail, then swap over the injectors and the top seals, applying petroleum jelly to all the seals.

4. Disconnect the breather pipe between the plenum and camshaft cover. Bung the end on the plenum and fit a filter on the cam cover. Fit a second filter on the breather connection on the other side of the cam cover.

5. A programmable ECU should be fitted to make the most of the supercharger conversion. The Megasquirt MS2 ECU shown here is a direct plug and play, which can then be fine-tuned. Depending on the model and year of MX-5, there are a number of different programmable ECUs available.

6. The MAF sensor isn't required, but the air temperature sensor on the Mk2 MX-5 will need to be fitted into a rubber or silicone section of the induction pipework between the intercooler and the car's throttle body.

TURBOCHARGING

Fitting a turbocharger on to an MX-5 engine is just as popular as supercharging. This is another form of forced induction, which is driven by exhaust gases (supercharging is belt driven). There are a range of conversion kits available, which appear to have largely been developed in the USA and seem to be similarly priced to supercharger conversions. Home-made turbocharger conversions are also popular, with many people using parts from other vehicles and fabricating other components themselves.

The owner of this home-brewed turbo conversion made his own exhaust manifold and pipework

gearbox and differential

OIL CHANGES

The oil inside the gearbox and differential should be renewed at every 24,000 miles or two years. This sort of work can be done on a driveway by raising the vehicle on four axle stands, or using a pair of drive-on ramps and a couple of axle stands. However, if you have access to a pit, or a two- or four-post ramp, then this is much easier.

Draining the differential and gearbox oil is quite straight-forward because there's plenty of space. Refilling the gearbox oil isn't quite so easy because there's a limited amount of space around the refill hole on the side of the gearbox. A 1-litre squeezy bottle is possibly the best method for topping up, but this is still awkward because there's only sufficient room to squeeze in half a litre at a time. The MX-5's gearbox should require a couple of litres, so you may need to fill the bottle four times.

The recommended oil for the gearbox is 75W90 gear oil and SAE 90 GL5 for the differential. Some specialists stock fully synthetic SHC 75W90 oil for the differential.

TOOLBOX

- ◆ *Container for draining oil*
- ◆ *Gear oil squeezy bottle and nozzle (1 litre)*
- ◆ *Penetrating fluid*
- ◆ *Sockets: 10, 24mm*
- ◆ *Spanner: 14mm*

Time: 45 minutes
On your own? Yes

1. The underside of the gearbox has a cover that's secured with 10mm bolts. Spray over these bolts with penetrating fluid and anticipate that some of them will shear off. Remove the cover.

4. The inspection and refill hole is on the side of the gearbox. Undo the plug with a 14mm open-ended spanner. There's not a lot of room to manoeuvre a bottle to refill the gearbox with oil.

2. Draining the gearbox oil is easier than refilling it. There's a large 24mm drain plug on the underside. Carefully slacken this plug and have your container ready to catch the oil.

5. Using a 1-litre gear oil squeezy bottle and nozzle, pump the appropriate oil into the gearbox. It should need 2 litres, but stop filling when the oil level is just below the access hole.

3. After fully undoing the gearbox drain plug, 2 litres of sludgy oil will hopefully drain out. Leave it to run out for several minutes before cleaning and refitting the drain plug.

6. The diff oil is a lot easier to renew than the gearbox. The 24mm drain plug is on the back of the diff and the refill hole is a little higher up. One litre of old oil should drain out of the diff.

7. The squeezy bottle and nozzle can be used again to refill the diff. There's plenty of room to manoeuvre a bottle and squeeze the oil through until it starts to leak out.

8. If several of the 10mm bolts sheared off when removing the cover in step 1, they should be repaired (drill and tap), but if there's only one or two that are damaged, the cover can be secured with cable ties.

CLUTCH RENEWAL

If there's next to no pedal travel at the clutch, it's slipping or juddering, the release bearing is squealing, or there are other worrying clutch-related noises, then it's time to renew these components.

Renewing the clutch on the Mazda MX-5 requires the gearbox to be dropped down, so a ramp or pit is essential. Providing the propshaft remains attached, there will be no loss of gear oil, although it's a good opportunity to change it (*see* above).

When renewing the clutch, the release bearing should also be changed. It's also worthwhile inspecting the condition of the flywheel and the bearing in the centre of it. If small cracks are visible on the face of the flywheel where it

mates to the clutch friction plate, it should be renewed. If the bearing inside the flywheel is seized, renew it – a new bearing can be expensive, but second-hand replacements are known to last.

Other problems that can emerge concern the clutch slave cylinder. It can fail when it's disturbed during the clutch renewal if the slave cylinder's seal gets damaged upon removal over the rough and corroded surface it's fitted to. The only way to find out if it has failed is when you've reassembled the car and try to test drive it.

Set aside a full day to complete a clutch change. The following steps reveal what's involved and are divided into three sections covering the underneath, removing the gearbox and renewing the clutch.

TOOLBOX

- Brake cleaner
- Breaker bar
- Clutch alignment tool
- Grease (multi-purpose)
- Hammer
- Penetrating fluid
- Screwdrivers
- Sockets/spanners: 10–24mm
- Torque wrench
- Transmission jack
- Trim tool
- Two- or four-post ramp
- Tyre lever or long pry bar

Time: 4–5 hours
On your own? No

Preparation Work

1. Remove the large steel undertray that protects the gearbox (not the plastic undertray for the engine). It should be secured with four 10mm bolts, which may be seized and will require plenty of penetrating fluid.

2. The MX-5 is equipped with a number of brace bars. There's one across the underneath of the gearbox, which has to be removed. It's secured with two 17mm bolts that can shear off, so apply penetrating fluid first.

3. The clutch slave cylinder is secured to the side of the gearbox with two 12mm bolts. This is known to need replacing after removing it because it can get damaged and start to leak.

4. Carefully undo three 14mm nuts and bolts that hold the end of the exhaust manifold to the downpipe. If these shear, the manifold will need to be removed to drill them out, so apply penetrating fluid.

5. There's an exhaust mounting bracket close to the three bolts undone in the last step. It holds the exhaust onto the gearbox and so it has to be released by undoing two 19mm bolts.

6. Undo the two 16mm nuts that join the exhaust's mid-pipe to the longer pipe that's routed to the back of the car. This may be heavily corroded, so there's a risk the studs will shear.

7. Detach the exhaust system further towards the back of the car. There may be a connection in front of the mid-silencer, or only one connection where the rear silencer is attached.

8. The exhaust system can now be removed. Drop the front of the exhaust down at the downpipe, then manoeuvre the pipework out, including the mid-section. Space is required to remove the gearbox.

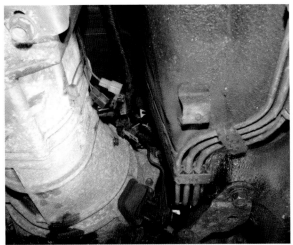

9. Detach the wiring connector plugs on the offside of the gearbox. There's also a mounting bracket for the wiring loom, which is attached to the side of the gearbox that needs to be undone, and an earth strap on the nearside.

10. Disconnect the battery, then undo the three 14mm bolts that secure the starter motor in position. The starter motor doesn't need to be removed, just the mounting bolts undone to separate it from the gearbox's bellhousing.

11. Undo the four 14mm bolts that secure the propshaft to the differential. Use a tyre lever or long pry bar to hold the propshaft and stop it rotating. Rotate the propshaft for easier access to each bolt.

12. The long aluminium power plant frame that runs alongside the propshaft has to be removed at the front, so undo the three 17mm bolts, then move it out of the way to ensure the gearbox can be removed later.

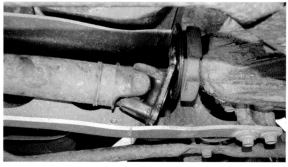

13. Detach the end of the propshaft from where it's fitted to the rear differential. Use a hammer and screwdriver to prise them apart. The propshaft will remain attached to the gearbox to avoid oil leaks.

14. Undo all of the 17mm bolts that secure the gearbox's bellhousing to the engine. A few of the bolts can be accessed from underneath the car, while the remaining ones can be located from within the engine bay.

Gearbox Removal

1. The centre console needs to be removed to access the mounting bolts for the gear lever. At the side of the console, prise off a clip and undo a crosshead mounting screw.

2. Lift the centre console compartment's lid and look for a couple of screws that secure this to the propshaft tunnel. Undo both of them.

3. Remove the compartment inside the ashtray and undo two more crosshead screws. Unscrew the gear knob and lift up the centre console, detaching the wiring plugs for the electric windows.

4. Undo four 12mm bolts that secure the gear lever surround to the propshaft tunnel. Prise off this surround and remove it. You will now be able to see where the gear lever sits in the gearbox.

5. Make sure neutral is selected, then carefully undo three 10mm bolts that secure the gear lever into the gearbox. When removing these bolts, don't drop them, although they will probably fall to the floor.

6. Lift out the gear lever and store it in a clean area. Avoid getting dirt on the end and dirt into where it's fitted in the gearbox. There should be a locating pin inside the gearbox, which helps when refitting the gear lever.

7. Position a transmission jack underneath the gearbox, then use a tyre lever to slowly prise it apart from the engine. Make sure the transmission jack can support the gearbox when it's released.

8. When the gearbox has been separated from the engine, ask someone to hold the propshaft (if it drops out of the gearbox, oil will leak out). Carefully manoeuvre the gearbox down to the ground.

Renewing the Clutch

1. Progressively undo the six 14mm bolts for the clutch plate, then remove it from the end of the flywheel on the engine. The friction plate can then be removed – note which way round it's fitted.

2. If you are renewing the clutch, look for a marking on the friction plate to indicate the gearbox side. If there are no markings, compare the new friction plate with the old one.

3. From within the bellhousing of the gearbox, remove the old clutch release bearing and clean inside this area with brake cleaner, wiping out the dirt with paper towels.

4. Apply multi-purpose grease to the area where the clutch release bearing was fitted, making sure all traces of dirt have been removed. Fit a new clutch release bearing.

5. Inspect the condition of the flywheel on the engine. If there are cracks in the mating surface where the clutch sits, it should be renewed. Undo the six 19mm bolts to remove it.

6. Another reason for removing the flywheel is to renew its bearing, especially if it is seized. This can be drifted out using a hammer and a suitable sized socket (24mm).

7. Refit the flywheel if it was removed, progressively tighten the six 19mm bolts in a diagonal pattern, then tighten them to 100Nm with a torque wrench. Lock the flywheel with a tyre lever to stop it rotating.

8. A clutch alignment tool can be used to fit the new friction and clutch plates, but a ratchet wrapped in masking tape and a torch to inspect the alignment are just as good.

9. Once the new clutch is in position and you've checked that it is correctly aligned, the gearbox can be refitted. Watch the propshaft doesn't drop out. Refit all remaining parts and be prepared to renew the clutch slave cylinder.

brake maintenance

SERVICE AND INSPECTION

The MX-5 uses a dual circuit braking system with servo assistance, single-piston calipers all round and in some cases, an anti-lock braking system (ABS). The brake fluid should be renewed every two years and the brakes should ideally be inspected and cleaned at least once a year.

A visual inspection of the brakes helps to determine that the brake discs are sufficiently thick and not too rusty, and that the outer brake pad hasn't worn to the limit, but the best approach is to strip the brakes down in order to thoroughly inspect and clean them. This can take a couple of hours, but it's worthwhile and will help to preserve your brakes should they start to bind.

Clean all of the sides of each brake pad with a wire brush.

Undo the slider bolts to remove the brake caliper and extract the brake pads.

The brake pads on the MX-5 can only be removed by removing the brake caliper. This involves undoing at least one of the slider bolts to enable the caliper to be levered out of the way. On the front there are two slider bolts, and it's worth undoing both of them so you can clean them. On the rear there's a lower slider bolt with a 10mm head, but the upper slider bolt is part of the caliper carrier.

Once the brake caliper is out of the way, the brake pads can be extracted, inspected and, if they are in a satisfactory condition to be used again, cleaned with a wire brush. When inspecting the brake pads, look for signs of uneven wear, damage to the braking surface and most important of all, a sufficient thickness of braking material. The minimum thickness of the braking material must be 1.5mm in the UK to pass the MOT test. This can be measured with a ruler, tyre tread depth gauge or vernier calipers. If one or more of the brake pads has worn below the limit or is damaged, all four brake pads across an axle must be renewed. So, for example, if only one of the front brake pads is worn excessively, all four brake pads on both of the front brakes must be renewed. This will help to ensure even braking across the front brakes.

The area where the brake pads are fitted is known as the caliper carrier, and this should be cleaned with a wire brush to remove any dirt that can contaminate the brakes. Similarly, the inside of the brake caliper can be cleaned, but avoid damaging the dust cover around the piston.

The edge of the brake disc will probably be covered in rust, but this can be cleaned off with a flat file or screwdriver to reduce the risk of any rust particles becoming trapped between the brake pads and the disc.

With a little practice, cleaning the brake pads, slider bolts, brake disc, caliper and carrier takes 15–20 minutes per corner (including removing and refitting the road wheel). Always spray over the brakes with brake cleaner to help remove any dirt.

Lift up the brake caliper to extract the brake pads.

After cleaning the brakes, apply some multi-purpose grease to the slider bolts and a small smear of copper grease to the top and bottom edges of the brake pads (not the braking surface) to reduce the risk of these components seizing and sticking.

Whenever you work on the brakes, always pump the brake pedal afterwards to ensure you have braking pressure, especially before setting off in the car.

BINDING BRAKES

A lack of maintenance can result in the MX-5's brakes binding. This not only reduces the performance of the vehicle, but risks overheating the brakes. If you suspect the brakes are binding, try driving the car for a few minutes and avoid braking. Stop the car, then put your hand close to the brakes (do not touch them as they may be hot) to feel whether they are warm. If one or more of the brakes is noticeably warmer than the rest, then further investigation is required.

The cause of binding brakes can be as straightforward as dirt and brake dust building up around the brake pads, but it can also be down to a seized slider bolt or a seized piston inside the brake caliper.

The best solution is to strip the brakes to clean the pads, slider bolts and caliper carrier, and test that the piston inside the brake caliper is free to move. This can be done by asking someone to carefully press the brake pedal while you watch the piston. If it moves out, make sure it doesn't go too far. Whether it moves out or not, spray some penetrating fluid down the sides of it (inside the dust cover), then push the piston back in using a G-clamp. Repeat this a few times to ensure the piston is free to move.

Unfortunately, in some cases the best solution for a brake caliper where the piston has seized is to renew it. A seized piston is often corroded, and while penetrating fluid will fix it in the short term, the rust isn't going to go away.

TOOLBOX

- ◆ **Brake cleaner**
- ◆ **Copper grease**
- ◆ **Emery paper**
- ◆ **G-clamp**
- ◆ **Multi-purpose grease**
- ◆ **Penetrating fluid**
- ◆ **Pry bar**
- ◆ **Sockets/spanners: 10–17mm**
- ◆ **Trolley jack and axle stands**
- ◆ **Wire brush**

Time: 1 hour
On your own? Yes

1. After raising a corner of the MX-5 and removing the road wheel, try to rotate the brake disc (make sure the handbrake is off and the gear lever is in neutral if working on the rear brake). If the brake disc is difficult to rotate, there is clearly a problem here.

2. On the front brakes, undo the upper and lower slider bolts (14mm and 17mm heads) and extract them. On the rear brakes, there's one 10mm bolt to undo for the lower slider bolt (the upper slider bolt is part of the caliper carrier).

3. Remove the brake caliper and suspend it without overstretching the flexi-hose. If necessary, use a pry bar for extra leverage. On the rear, try moving the caliper up and down to free it off the upper slider bolt.

4. Extract the brake pads. Use a wire brush to clean around the caliper carrier, inside the caliper and the edges of the brake pads. Spray over all of these components with brake cleaner to remove any remaining dirt.

7. Spray penetrating fluid inside the piston and its dust cover to help free it off or at least reduce the risk of it seizing. Press the brake pedal once or twice to see if the piston moves (don't push it out too far), then repeat the last step to push it in.

5. Make sure the slider bolts are clean. Use a strip of emery paper to remove any dirt and corrosion. Apply some multi-purpose grease to the smooth surfaces of the slider bolts to reduce the risk of them seizing.

8. If you are satisfied the piston in the caliper isn't seized, reassemble the brakes, applying a smear of copper grease to the top and bottom edges of the brake pads (not the braking surface).

NEW DISCS AND PADS

If a brake disc has worn down to the limit, or it's heavily corroded, then the best solution is to renew both sides. Brake discs must be renewed in pairs (both fronts or both rears) and new brake pads must always be fitted.

Bedding in brakes is also important. In most cases, avoid harsh braking for the first 100–200 miles. This also applies when fitting new brake pads – allow time for the brake pads to wear down a little without getting too hot.

The work involved in renewing the brake discs and pads on the MX-5 is very similar on the front and rear. The section covering ABS repairs, which is later in this chapter, shows how to remove the discs and pads on the front of the MX-5, so the photographs accompanying this section show a rear disc and set of pads being renewed. The major differences concern the slider bolts and the adjustment of a handbrake stop on the rear calipers, which can prevent the caliper being refitted with new discs and pads that are thicker than the ones being replaced.

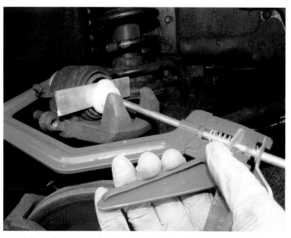

6. After checking the brake fluid level to make sure it isn't too high, use a G-clamp to push the piston in the brake caliper inwards and check that it isn't seized. If it has seized, see the next step for more help.

Time: 2–4 hours
On your own? Yes

3. On the rear brakes, the caliper may need to be moved up and down to ease it off the upper slider bolt. This slider bolt is part of the caliper carrier and, if it's corroded, it will be difficult to free off.

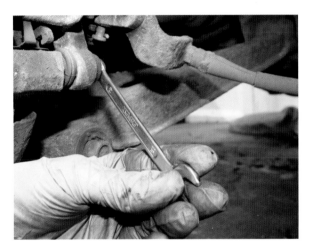

1. Start by undoing the slider bolt(s). On the front brakes there are upper and lower slider bolts, whereas on the rear there's only one lower slider bolt. Once undone, extract the slider bolts and make sure they are clean.

4. The brake flexi-hose or ABS sensor wiring may get in the way of the next step, when the caliper carrier has to be removed, so undo any mounting brackets nearby that seem to be in the way.

2. Remove the brake caliper and suspend it aside with a bungee or something similar – don't overstretch the flexi-hose. If the caliper is difficult to remove, use a pry bar for extra leverage.

5. Extract the brake pads and discard them – new brake discs must be fitted with new pads. Undo the two bolts at the back of the caliper carrier, which secure it in position. These will be difficult to undo, so use a breaker bar.

6. Once both of the caliper carrier bolts have been undone, the caliper carrier can be removed. This is a good opportunity to clean the carrier thoroughly. The brake pads sit here and don't want to be contaminated with dirt.

9. Clean the disc guard, which often corrodes and deposits rust on the brakes. If you have time, it can be painted with a suitable metal paint to help prevent corrosion recurring.

7. The brake disc can now be removed. Check there are no retaining screws between the wheel studs. The brake disc probably won't fall off when you try to remove it, so hit it with a lump hammer (wear safety goggles).

10. Compare the old brake disc with the new one, making sure it's the same size and has the same mounting holes. Spray brake cleaner over the new disc to remove any protective oil that's been applied to prevent corrosion.

8. Use a wire brush to clean the mating surface on the hub where the brake disc sits. This will help to reduce the risk of the new brake disc seizing to the mating surface in the future and being difficult to remove.

11. The new brake disc will probably rust in the future, but this can be prevented by applying a high-temperature paint to the areas where the brake pads do not touch, such as the outer edge and the middle section.

12. Fit the new brake disc, followed by the caliper carrier. Fit a new pair of brake pads, applying a smear of copper grease to the top and bottom edges. Refit the brake caliper.

13. If the brake pads refuse to be fitted into the carrier, the paint on the top and bottom edges may need filing down a little to make room. The brake pads sit inside spring clips, so they can be awkward to fit.

14. If the brake caliper cannot be fitted over the new brake disc and pads, the piston will need to be pushed in. Check the brake fluid level in the reservoir, then use a G-clamp to force the piston in.

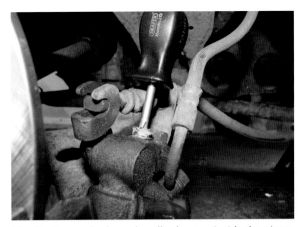

15. On the rear brakes, a handbrake stop inside the piston may need to be wound out a little to allow the piston to be pushed in sufficiently to refit the caliper. Look at the back of the caliper for a plastic plug and extract it.

16. The handbrake stop for the rear calipers consists of a 4mm Allen key bolt. Unwind it a little, then try to refit the brake caliper by repeating step 14. If successful, refit the plug and reassemble the brakes. Pump the brake pedal before driving the car.

HANDBRAKE ADJUSTMENT

The mechanical handbrake on the MX-5 operates the rear calipers. There are two methods of adjustment; one at the handbrake and another at each of the calipers.

On the back of each rear caliper there should be a plastic plug to unscrew, which, when removed, reveals a 4mm Allen key bolt inside. This acts as a stop against the piston and controls the movement of it, which in turn alters the handbrake. The stop shouldn't be wound in too far because this can cause the brakes to bind. However, it also shouldn't be wound out too much because the handbrake and brakes may then not be effective. With the handbrake off, try winding the stop in, but keep rotating the respective rear wheel to make sure the brakes are not binding.

The handbrake cable can be adjusted at the base of the handbrake lever. Remove any plastic trim from around the handbrake lever to see the end of the handbrake cable, which can be adjusted using a flat-blade screwdriver. Make sure the handbrake is down (off) when adjusting the cable. You should be able to pull the lever up by roughly six clicks, whereby the rear brakes will be locked.

TOOLBOX

- ◆ **Allen key tool: 4mm**
- ◆ **Screwdrivers**
- ◆ **Trolley jack and axle stands**

Time: 1 hour
On your own? Yes

1. The back of each rear caliper should have a plastic plug, which can be removed to reveal a 4mm Allen key bolt. Wind it in until the rear brake disc stops rotating, then back it off at least a quarter of a turn.

2. After adjusting the rear calipers, remove any trim around the base of the handbrake lever inside the car. The panel shown here is secured with a single cross-head screw.

3. With the handbrake off, adjust the end of the cable with a flat-blade screwdriver. Aim for around six clicks of the lever when pulling it upwards before the handbrake fully locks both rear wheels.

4. Test the handbrake several times after adjusting it. Test drive the car and make sure the rear brakes are not binding (avoid braking and check they are not hot).

BRAKE CALIPER RENEWAL

The MX-5's single piston calipers can seize if the piston becomes corroded inside, and the handbrake mechanism at the rear can become similarly troublesome. Often the easiest solution is to fit a new caliper, and they are reasonably straightforward to change. On the front there are a couple of slider bolts to undo and the brake flexi-hose before the caliper can be swapped over. At the rear, the handbrake mechanism has to be detached before you can remove the caliper.

A problem that can arise when renewing a caliper is the brake fluid that will leak out of the flexi-hose and the old caliper. This is corrosive, so wipe up any spills and keep the fluid away from the car's paintwork as it will damage it.

If the new caliper cannot fit over the brake pads, check whether its piston needs to be pushed in with a G-clamp. This problem can occur on the rear brakes, where pushing the piston in won't help to fit the caliper and clear the brake pads. Instead, the stop in the back of the caliper may need to be adjusted to fit

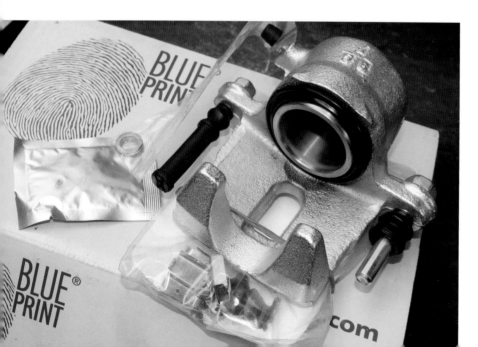

the caliper over the brake pads. The stop helps with hand-brake adjustment, controlling the movement of the piston inside the caliper. It's covered by a plastic plug, but once that's removed, you will find a 4mm Allen key bolt inside. Try winding the bolt out a little, then push the piston back with the G-clamp and see if the caliper can be fitted over the brake pads.

The banjo bolt that secures the end of the brake flexi-hose to the brake caliper must be refitted with a pair of new copper washers. These washers are crushed by the banjo bolt, helping to achieve a liquid tight seal, so do not reuse old ones. After renewing the caliper and bleeding the brakes, always look for leaks from around the banjo bolt.

TOOLBOX

- ◆ *Allen key: 4, 10mm*
- ◆ *Brake bleeder*
- ◆ *Brake clamp or flat-jawed vice grips*
- ◆ *Copper and multi-purpose grease*
- ◆ *Emery paper*
- ◆ *Hammer*
- ◆ *Length of wood*
- ◆ *Penetrating fluid*
- ◆ *Safety goggles*
- ◆ *Screwdrivers and pry bar*
- ◆ *Sockets/spanners: 10–17mm*
- ◆ *Trolley jack and axle stands*
- ◆ *Wire brush*

Time: 1 hour
On your own? Yes

Front Brake Caliper

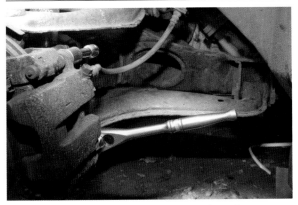

1. Slacken the respective wheel nuts, raise a front corner of the car and support with an axle stand, then remove the road wheel. Undo the upper and lower 14mm and 17mm slider bolts, which will allow the caliper to be removed.

2. Slacken the 12mm banjo bolt that attaches the brake flexi-hose to the caliper. This is easier to slacken with the brake caliper fitted than wrestling with it after the caliper has been removed.

3. Brake fluid will leak out when the brake flexi-hose is detached from the caliper, so clamp the hose to stop fluid escaping. Flat-jawed vice grips are ideal if you haven't got a proper clamp.

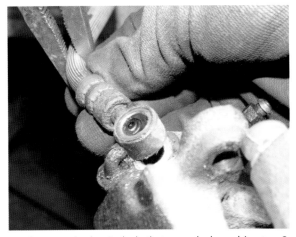

4. Remove the banjo bolt that was slackened in step 2, then remove the flexi-hose where it is attached to the caliper. It has a locating peg, which may be corroded and will require a little waggling.

5. Remove the old brake caliper – you may need to use a pry bar to lever it off. Brake fluid will leak out, so wipe up any spillage and avoid getting the fluid on to the car's paintwork, as it will damage it.

7. Refit the flexi-hose to the new caliper with two new copper washers, ensuring the locating peg sits inside the hole in the caliper. This stops the flexi-hose moving when the steering is turned.

8. The brake caliper will need bleeding to ensure it's full of brake fluid and doesn't contain any air. The photograph here shows a brake bleeder that's attached to an air compressor to allow the brake fluid to be sucked through.

6. Trial fit the new caliper. The lower slider bolt can be fitted to the caliper, allowing it to be fitted into the caliper carrier. Apply grease to the smooth surface of both slider bolts. New slider bolts should be supplied with the new caliper.

Rear Brake Caliper

1. The handbrake mechanism on the rear calipers can seize up, resulting in a weak handbrake and an MOT failure. The piston's dust cover can perish, as shown here, which will eventually result in corrosion of the piston and seizure. The following steps show how to renew a rear caliper.

4. Undo the 14mm mounting bolt that secures the handbrake cable to the back of the caliper. Once undone, detach the end of the handbrake cable from the caliper and suspend it out of the way so that the caliper can be removed later.

2. The rear of the MX-5 can be raised by placing a trolley jack underneath the diff casing, but the vehicle must be supported by axle stands placed under the rear of the side sills or the rear subframe. Do not rely upon the trolley jack.

5. Undo the 10mm lower slider bolt for the brake caliper. There is no upper slider bolt to undo. Extract the lower slider bolt and check its condition. If it's corroded, clean it with emery paper. It will be lubricated before being refitted.

3. Try to slacken the 12mm banjo bolt that connects the brake flexi-hose to the brake caliper. Once slackened, do not undo it any further, but nip it up so that brake fluid doesn't leak out. You merely need to be certain that the banjo bolt can be undone at this stage.

6. Try to lever the caliper upwards to see if it can be manoeuvred off the upper slider. The brake flexi-hose is still attached, so the caliper cannot be fully removed yet. If the caliper is stiff to move, lever it up and down to work it loose.

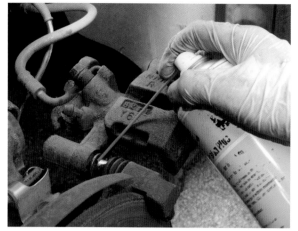

7. If the caliper is very stiff to move up and down, it may prove difficult to separate from the upper slider. Try applying some penetrating fluid to the upper slider and work the caliper up and down to see if this helps.

10. Don't remove any plastic bungs from the new brake caliper, but make sure they are loose. Fit the new brake caliper over the upper slider. Lever it up and down and in and out to make sure it moves freely.

8. Clamp the brake flexi-hose to prevent brake fluid loss, then undo the banjo bolt for the brake flexi-hose, which was slackened in step 3. Remove the old caliper off the end of the upper slider.

11. Line up the mounting hole for the lower slider bolt and refit the slider bolt that was extracted in step 5. Make sure the bolt is lubricated with multi-purpose grease (or use the grease supplied with the caliper).

9. Check the condition of the brake pads and disc. Clean the upper slider and the lower slider bolts with emery paper, then apply multi-purpose grease to help lubricate them. Grease may be supplied with the new caliper.

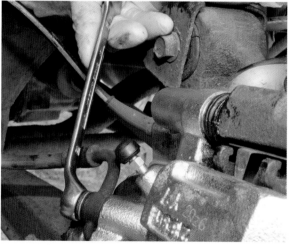

12. Refit the handbrake cable and its 14mm bolt into the new caliper. Remove the old copper washers from the end of the brake flexi-hose's banjo bolt and refit it with two new copper washers. Bleed the brakes.

BRAKE PIPE RENEWAL

If a brake pipe has become corroded to the extent that it's breaking down, it will not only fail the MOT test, but is also at risk of leaking brake fluid, so it's worthwhile renewing either a section of it or the entire length. The brake pipes on the MX-5 are accessible and can be renewed by undoing their connections to extract a complete length of pipe. The rear brake pipes are accessed from underneath the car, whereas the front pipes are routed within the engine bay.

There are a number of methods for renewing a brake pipe. Some people prefer to renew an entire length of pipework, which helps to retain the integrity of the brake pipes. Others choose to renew only a section that is corroded or damaged, which entails making flared ends in situ.

After renewing a brake pipe, the brakes must be bled to remove any air in the system. However, brake fluid should be renewed every two years because it absorbs moisture (hygroscopic), which leads to corrosion inside the brake system, resulting in leaks and rust particles damaging the seals.

TOOLBOX

◆ **Brake bleeder**
◆ **Brake cleaner**
◆ **Brake pipe flaring tool**
◆ **Brake pipe spanner**
◆ **Length of wood or pry bar**
◆ **Penetrating fluid**
◆ **String**

Time: 1 hour
On your own? Yes

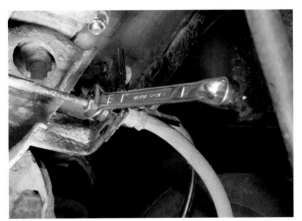

1. Try to undo the brake pipe at a connection (for example a pipe nut), using either a brake pipe spanner or a suitable open-ended spanner. Spray penetrating fluid over the connection first. Alternatively, cut the pipe at the connection, then use a socket to undo it.

2. After detaching or cutting through a brake pipe, brake fluid will leak out. Press the brake pedal down and wedge a length of wood or a long pry bar against it. This will reduce the amount of brake fluid that leaks out.

3. When removing an old length of brake pipe that you intend to replace, use it as a template for the new pipe, so try to retain its shape and length. Remember where the pipe is clipped into position and make sure these fixings are in good condition.

4. With the old brake pipe removed, measure its length with a piece of string, then make up the same length with new pipework. Add suitable pipe nut connections and flare the ends using a flaring tool.

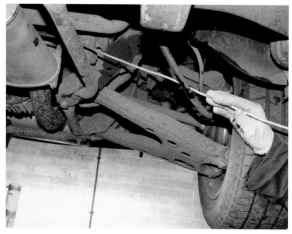

5. Carefully feed the new brake pipe into position on the underside of the vehicle. Try to manoeuvre it into position and line it up with any clips or other methods of securing it to the vehicle.

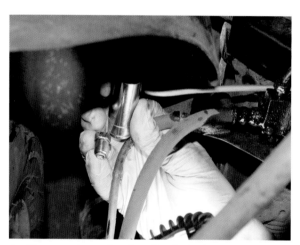

6. If you need to make a bend in the brake pipe, use something round, such as a large socket or jam jar, to avoid kinking the pipe. If you kink the pipe, this could restrict brake fluid, meaning you will have to discard it.

7. Once the brake pipe is roughly in position, make sure the ends can be connected to the respective points on the vehicle (junctions, flexi-pipes and other pipes). Carefully tighten each connection, making sure it doesn't become cross-threaded.

8. Wash all areas where brake fluid has leaked, especially over paintwork (most types of brake fluid will corrode paintwork). Spray brake cleaner over the connections to clean and dry them, then bleed the brakes and check for leaks.

ABS TROUBLE

A common problem on the MX-5 is ABS sensor failure. The first sign of this is when the ABS light appears on the dashboard; in some cases, it appears on some days and doesn't on others. The problem doesn't fix itself, however, and eventually the light stays permanently illuminated.

One possible solution is to clean the reluctor ring and sensor at the back of each hub using a soft brush. Sometimes dirt and light corrosion can affect the sensor, resulting in the warning light appearing on the dashboard. Sadly, this remedy doesn't always help, so the next solution is to connect a diagnostic unit to find the cause of the fault. Depending on the diagnostic unit being used, the ABS light on the dashboard may start to flash. Count the number of flashes to establish the cause of the fault.

In many cases, sensor failure is to blame. The best solution is to replace the sensor, but removing it from the hub is usually very difficult. The 12mm bolt that secures it to the back of the hub will probably shear off and the sensor will feel as though it has been welded in position. There's not much room to drift it out, and new sensors can be very expensive. The cheaper solution is to buy a second-hand hub from a scrapyard, which includes a sensor that has been tested with a multi-meter. Even if you do buy a new sensor, you may still have to remove the hub in order to extract the old sensor!

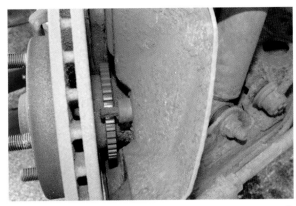 

Cleaning the end of the ABS sensor and the reluctor ring can sometimes fix an ABS warning light problem.

Plugging in a diagnostic unit should help identify the cause of an ABS problem. You may have to count the number of times the ABS light flashes on the dashboard.

Before purchasing a second-hand hub, inspect the sensor's wiring and make sure you source a hub with the same length and layout. In some cases, the wiring is longer and has more fixings for mounting it to the inner wheelarch.

If a second-hand hub is sourced from a reputable scrapyard, it should have a limited guarantee to ensure the ABS sensor is working properly. However, it may also be supplied with the remains of the suspension arms and track rod end still attached. Scrapyards cannot afford to waste time detaching ball joints, so they will slice through suspension arms and track rod ends with an angle grinder or similar cutting tool. Consequently, you will need to detach these amputated components by splitting their respective ball joints. All of this is outlined in the next six steps, followed by a guide to removing a front hub assembly from the MX-5 and fitting its replacement second-hand unit.

Buying a second-hand hub with a working ABS sensor is often cheaper than buying a new sensor.

There are two types of ABS sensor at the front of the MX-5. The difference is in the length of the wiring and its fixing points.

TOOLBOX

- ◆ *Ball joint splitter*
- ◆ *Blowtorch*
- ◆ *Breaker bar*
- ◆ *Drift*
- ◆ *Goggles and gloves*
- ◆ *Hammer*
- ◆ *Penetrating fluid*
- ◆ *Pliers*
- ◆ *Pry bar*
- ◆ *Scissor jack*
- ◆ *Sockets/spanners: 10–21mm*
- ◆ *Soft brush*
- ◆ *Trolley jack and axle stands*
- ◆ *Vice grips*

Time: 4–6 hours
On your own? Yes

3. Once a split pin has been removed, try to undo the castle nut. Secure the hub in a vice and use a suitable socket and breaker bar. Most ball joint nuts are 17mm and 21mm on the MX-5's suspension arms and track rod end.

Stripping Down a Second-Hand Hub

1. If you've sourced another hub from a scrapyard then it may be supplied with the amputated suspension arms and track rod end still attached, so these ball joints will need to be removed. Start by spraying over the respective nuts with penetrating fluid.

4. After undoing the nuts for the suspension ball joints and track rod end, the ball joint will need to be separated from the hub/upright. Try using a hammer to hit the part of the hub where the ball joint is fitted to shock it into releasing.

2. If split pins have been fitted to retain the ball joints' securing nuts (castle nuts) then these will need to be extracted. They will probably be rusty, so use pliers, vice grips, drifts and screwdrivers to pull them free.

5. If the ball joint fails to release after hitting the hub, try using a ball joint splitter. There are a number of different types that can be used, including ones that can be wound in to release the ball joint and the fork type that requires a hammer.

6. If a ball joint splitter fails to separate the old ball joint from the hub/upright, heat may be the answer. Using a hand-held blowtorch, warm up the hub/upright around the ball joint's thread, then hit it with a hammer or use a ball joint splitter.

2. Prise the caliper off and secure it on the suspension's lower arm to avoid overstretching the brake flexi-hose. If the caliper cannot be removed, use a pry bar to push the piston in a little and lever the caliper off.

7. Make sure the ABS sensor and reluctor ring are clean. Use a soft brush to remove any dirt, which can affect how the sensor operates. Also, check that the reluctor ring isn't damaged and that the sensor is secure.

3. Remove the brake pads along with any retaining clips (remember how they were fitted). The brake pads may need to be carefully levered out with a screwdriver, but avoid damaging them and breaking bits off.

Removing a Front Hub

1. Raise a front corner of the car and support with an axle stand. Remove the road wheel and undo the 14mm and 17mm slider bolts for the brakes. Extract these bolts and store them aside in a clean area.

4. Look at the ABS sensor wire and undo its mounting point nearest the brake. This will give you more room for the next step. The mounting point will probably be a 12mm bolt and bracket – spray penetrating fluid over the bolt.

5. Undo the two 14mm caliper carrier mounting bolts. These will be very tight, so use a long breaker bar to undo them. You may need to carefully turn the steering for better access. Take your time with this.

8. If the disc refuses to come off, you may have to resort to hitting the back of it with a lump hammer. Wear goggles and gloves and rotate the disc after hitting it. Ideally, a puller should be used but most mechanics use a hammer.

6. Once both caliper carrier bolts have been undone, the carrier can be removed. It will probably need a thorough clean, but don't lose any clips fitted to it, which are for the brake pads.

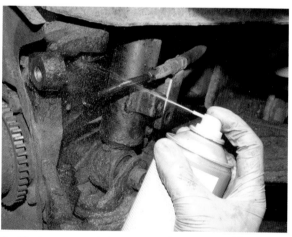

9. You're now ready to separate the upper and lower ball joints and the track rod end, and then remove the hub. First spray penetrating fluid over the castle nuts for these three ball joints.

7. The brake disc can now be removed. There may be a securing screw to undo on the face of the disc, but if there's only a small hole there isn't anything to undo. Try to waggle the disc until it releases.

10. Extract the split pins for the upper and lower ball joints and the track rod end. This can be awkward and the split pin may break up, so ensure enough of it is removed to be able to undo the castle nut.

11. After extracting all the split pins, the next job can be just as difficult. The three 17mm and 21mm castle nuts need to be undone. Slacken all three before fully undoing them. Use a breaker bar and extensions to help.

14. The lower ball joint is bolted to the lower arm in two places. First, undo the 17mm nut and bolt that secures the bottom of the damper to the lower suspension arm. This will provide more room to undo one of the ball joint's mounting bolts.

12. You will probably want to avoid renewing the ball joints and track rod end, so don't use a ball joint splitter to release them. Instead, use a hammer to hit the side of the upright where the ball joint is fed through. This will shock and release it.

15. A 17mm nut and bolt fits through the bottom arm and ball joint. These are straightforward to undo and extract, but there's one more bolt to undo before the ball joint can be released, and this is covered in the next step.

13. The bottom ball joint for the lower suspension arm can be difficult to release as the weight of the hub is bearing down on it. If hitting the side of it with a hammer doesn't work, the hub can be removed with its ball joint – *see* the next four steps.

16. Pull down on the lower suspension arm and move the base of the damper away from it. There should be enough space to squeeze a 17mm socket in and undo the ball joint's final securing bolt.

17. Finally the hub can be released from the suspension arms. However, the ABS sensor wiring is still attached, so don't go too far with it. Instead, reposition it into its ball joints and proceed with detaching the wiring.

19. Trace the ABS wire through into the engine bay and find the end of it. There will be a plug connector, but you may need to remove a section of induction pipe-work first to see it and to feed the wire through to the wheelarch.

18. Undo any remaining mounting bolts inside the inner wheelarch that secure the ABS sensor wire. These will probably be a mixture of 10mm and 12mm bolts and can easily shear off, so apply penetrating fluid.

20. Detach the plastic plug connector for the ABS wire (usually a push-in type), then feed the ABS wire through into the wheelarch, using a screwdriver to prise out the grommet, which may be a little brittle and hard.

21. The hub can now be removed from the car. Take this opportunity to clean and inspect the suspension components left behind. Make sure the threads for the ball joints that are being reused are clean.

Fitting a Replacement Hub

1. Before fitting a replacement hub, compare old and new together to make sure you have the right one. Clean any threads on the replacement hub and make sure the ABS sensor wire doesn't get damaged.

2. One potential issue when fitting the hub is tightening the castle nuts for the ball joints. If the ball joint's thread starts to spin, especially the track rod end, try raising it a little with a scissor jack to put some load on it.

3. Don't forget to fit new split pins after fitting the castle nuts and line up the holes. Do not reuse old split pins. After refitting everything, you may need to drive the car to ensure the ABS warning light doesn't remain illuminated.

brake upgrades

When you're considering modifying a car, the brakes are one of the most important aspects. After all, the faster you can make a car go, the better it needs to stop. However, brake modifications are only worthwhile if components such as the tyres and suspension are in good condition. Old tyres with worn tread won't get the most out of a modified brake set-up, and neither will tired suspension springs and dampers that fail to absorb the undulations in the road when you're pressing hard on the brake pedal.

PERFORMANCE BRAKE PADS

One of the most popular ways to improve the MX-5's braking performance is to fit a set of performance brake pads.

Performance brake pads from specialists such as Mintex generally offer better braking over standard pads.

Manufacturers such as EBC and Mintex produce a wide range of these uprated pads, which can be fitted with standard brake discs. If you are only going to uprate one set of brake pads (the front set or the rear set), then always uprate the front brakes. This also applies to cars with uprated brake pads all round – as so often happens, when the front pads become worn you may decide to fit standard pads, but you will then need to fit standard pads on the rear.

Uprated brake pads are usually constructed with a braking material that provides a greater amount of grip. There was a time when many of these brake pads only made a noticeable difference when the brakes were warm or hot. This appears to be less of an issue nowadays, with products such as EBC's track and fast road YellowStuff pads, for instance, providing a good level of grip whether they are hot or cold. To get the most out of such brake pads, however, hard braking is essential. Repeated gentle braking can result in the discs and pads glazing over, which reduces their braking efficiency. This can often be resolved through hard braking to de-glaze them.

There is a downside to performance brake pads. They generally don't seem to last as long as standard brake pads, and they could also accelerate the wear of the brake disc. You can't get something for nothing.

Bedding in new brake pads is essential with all brake pads, whether they are standard or performance rated. Avoid harsh braking for at least the first 100 miles. During this time, the brake pads will usually bind against the brake disc and remain warm or hot until some friction material is worn away. Heavy braking will add to this heat and the brakes will not have the chance to cool down, unlike brakes that have already bedded in. This can result in overheating, boiled brake fluid and warped discs.

PERFORMANCE DISCS

Brake specialists, including Black Diamond, EBC, Rossini and Nitrac, manufacture a range of performance brake discs, but are they really any better than standard discs? Most brake discs are made from cast iron in a process that starts with molten metal being poured into a mould to make the shape of the disc. This is then machined to add any dimples, grooves and holes.

A performance brake disc differs from a standard disc in how it dissipates heat and brake dust to maintain a high level of braking performance and avoid brake fade. When the brakes become hot the resin in the pads, which is used to hold the friction material to the backing material, overheats and turns to gas. If the resin's gas becomes trapped between the brake pad and disc, braking efficiency is reduced, which is known as brake fade.

Grooves in the brake disc collect brake dust and the aforementioned gas to channel it out so that it can escape. Dimples, holes and slots in the surface of the brake disc also provide an area for the brake dust and gas to collect.

Some brake manufacturers drill holes in their discs, whereas others prefer to add a dimple, believing that a hole all the way through increases the risk of fractures.

The cooling benefits of drilled and grooved discs are

EBC's turbo groove discs and YellowStuff pads are suitable for road and track use.

generally not appreciated under normal road use. It's only when a car is constantly undergoing heavy braking, such as on a race circuit, that a drilled and grooved disc will prolong the time before brake fade emerges.

In most cases uprated brake discs are no larger than standard discs and their accompanying brake pads cannot provide a greater braking surface. This is because the brake disc size is restricted by the capacity of the brake caliper and the space available to mount the brake disc.

COOLING

To get the best performance from the MX-5's standard brakes they generally shouldn't be too cold or too hot. If the brakes become too hot, problems associated with brake fade and boiling brake fluid can arise. If the brakes remain too cold, then the braking efficiency may not be as good as if the brakes were warm.

Some road wheels are designed to draw air into the brakes, which is similar to how the front-vented brake discs on the MX-5 provide a cooling effect.

Ducting can be fixed underneath the front of the car to direct air to the brakes, and some spoilers are designed to channel air to the brakes.

The steel disc guard protects the back of the disc from road dirt, but this can interfere with cooling so it can be removed. This isn't recommended for road use, however, where the brake discs can become contaminated with road dirt, resulting in corrosion and a loss of braking efficiency.

HOW TO CHECK RUNOUT

A brake disc that rotates true (straight) will reduce the risk of uneven braking and brake judder, provides less unwanted friction (rolling resistance) and saves on excessive brake wear. From a driving point of view, the car will feel smoother and the brakes will feel more responsive.

To ensure a brake disc is rotating true the best answer is to measure the runout, which is the amount the brake disc is moving from left to right when it's rotating. A dial gauge can be used to measure this. Most brake manufacturers recommend anything up to 0.15mm, although some performance brake specialists seem to set a lower limit of between 0.06mm and 0.1mm.

TOOLBOX

- ◆ *Brake cleaner*
- ◆ *Breaker bar*
- ◆ *Dial gauge with magnetic stand*
- ◆ *Emery paper*
- ◆ *Flat file*
- ◆ *Lump hammer*
- ◆ *Safety goggles*
- ◆ *Sockets/spanners: 10–17mm*
- ◆ *Trolley jack and axle stands*
- ◆ *Washers*
- ◆ *Wheel brace*

Time: 1–2 hours
On your own? Yes

Excessive runout can be an indication that a brake disc has warped, but it's first worth checking the brake disc is mated flat against the hub. If the runout of a brake disc is excessive, start by removing it, then clean the mating surface of the hub and inside the brake disc where it sits against the hub. If this reduces the amount of runout then you've found the answer. Otherwise, inspect the brake disc with a straight edge to see if it's warped and also check the mating surface of the hub with a straight edge.

2. Secure a magnetic dial gauge stand into the upper suspension arm, then adjust the dial gauge so that it is touching the face of the brake disc. Turn the brake disc and note how far the needle moves.

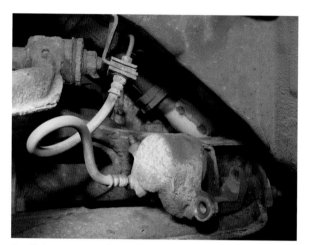

3. If the amount of runout is greater than recommended, the brake disc should be removed to clean the mating surface on the hub. First, undo the two slider bolts (one at the rear), extract the caliper and rest it on the lower suspension arm.

1. Raise and support a corner of the car and remove the road wheel. The brake disc may seem to be securely fitted, but the wheel and its bolts do this, so refit the wheel nuts with washers.

4. Remove the brake pads, undo the two caliper carrier bolts (use a breaker bar as they will be tight) and remove the carrier. Finally, remove the brake disc. If it's seized on to the hub, gently tap around the back of it with a lump hammer.

5. With the brake disc removed, clean inside it where it sits against the hub. Rust may have built up here, which can affect how true the brake disc rotates. Cleaning here will also help to make it easier to remove the disc in the future.

6. Clean the mating surface of the hub with emery paper and a flat file. This includes the outer edge shown here, and around the wheel studs. Refit the brake disc and secure it with washers and wheel nuts, then measure the runout again.

FOUR-POT CALIPERS

The MX-5's standard single-piston calipers can only be modified so far with performance brake discs and pads before you find you're looking for even more stopping power. The best solution in such a situation is to fit multi-piston brake calipers. Performance brake manufacturers such as HiSpec, AP Racing, Wilwood and Brembo produce a range of multi-piston calipers. These uprated brakes are usually fitted to the front, where most of the braking effort is required; the rear brakes are deemed to be sufficient in most cases.

The work involved in fitting multi-piston calipers to the front of the MX-5 includes the removal of the standard brake caliper, disc and pads. An adaptor bracket usually has to be fitted for the uprated brake caliper. This also allows the space to fit a larger-diameter aftermarket brake disc.

One of the common problems with uprating the front brakes with multi-piston calipers and larger brake discs concerns the wheels. In some cases, the standard wheels cannot be fitted because they foul the larger brakes, so check this before buying such brakes. Sometimes a set of spacers fitted behind the road wheels can solve the problem.

The following steps show the fitting of a second-hand pair of HiSpec four-pot brake calipers and aftermarket brake discs.

TOOLBOX

- ◆ *Allen key: 10mm*
- ◆ *Brake bleeder*
- ◆ *Brake clamp or vice grips*
- ◆ *Copper and multi-purpose grease*
- ◆ *Emery paper*
- ◆ *Hammer*
- ◆ *Length of wood*
- ◆ *Safety goggles*
- ◆ *Screwdrivers and pry bar*
- ◆ *Sockets/spanners: 10–17mm*
- ◆ *Trolley jack and axle stands*
- ◆ *Wire brush*

Time: 1–2 hours
On your own? Yes

3. The old brake disc can now be removed as it will not be required. It may be stuck against the mating surface of the hub. If this is the case, put on a pair of safety goggles and tap the back of the disc with a hammer to help release it.

1. The old front brakes need to be removed, including the caliper, carrier, disc and pads. Clamp the brake flexi-hose, undo the 12mm banjo bolt where the brake flexi-hose is attached to the caliper, then suspend the hose against the suspension.

4. Using a strip of emery paper, clean the mating surface of the hub where the old brake disc sat. This surface can be lightly coated in a small amount of copper grease before fitting the new brake disc.

2. Undo the two 14mm caliper carrier bolts (not the slider bolts) and remove the carrier and caliper together. It may help to use a pry bar to lever this assembly off, or lever against the brake pads and disc to push the caliper's piston in.

5. This particular four-pot caliper conversion from HiSpec includes a mounting bracket for the new caliper, which is bolted to the original caliper carrier mounting points on the MX-5's upright. The disc guard may need bending to avoid fouling it.

6. The new brake disc can now be fitted. It's not fitted to the hub with anything, but will remain secure once the road wheel is in position. Rotate the disc to check it doesn't foul the disc guard.

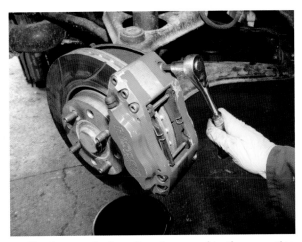

7. The four-pot brake caliper is secured to the mounting bracket fitted in step 5 using large 10mm Allen key-headed bolts. These must be secure, so it's worth fitting them with thread lock, but check with the manufacturer or supplier first.

8. In some cases the original brake flexi-hose can be refitted with new copper washers, but check it's not over-stretched when the steering is on full lock. The new brakes may be positioned further out on their new mountings, so a standard flexi-hose may be too short.

9. Once both new front brakes have been fitted, bleed them. There may be two bleed nipples on each caliper, so make sure both are slackened and bled through to help remove all traces of air from the system.

10. Refit the front road wheels, secure them with all of their wheel nuts and try to rotate them. Listen and feel for the wheel fouling the brake calipers. If this happens, you may need to fit spacers on to the hub or fit larger-diameter wheels.

UPRATED FLEXI-HOSES

The standard rubber flexi-hoses can be replaced with hoses that have a PTFE inner lining and a braided steel outer casing. Under hard braking, the standard rubber flexi-hoses can balloon a little, resulting in less braking effort being delivered to the brakes. Braided steel hoses offer less expansion, so the braking pressure is maintained. Braided steel brake flexi-hoses are manufactured by hose specialists such as Goodridge, Hose Technik and Hel, and stocked by most MX-5 and motorsport specialists.

Changing the brake flexi-hoses is a good opportunity to refresh the brake fluid, which should be changed every two years. Always fit new copper washers where the flexi-hose is attached to the brake caliper. After fitting the new flexi-hoses, bleed the brakes, then ask someone to press the brake pedal while you inspect all connections for fluid leaks.

TOOLBOX

- ◆ *Brake bleeder*
- ◆ *Clean cloths*
- ◆ *Length of wood*
- ◆ *Penetrating fluid*
- ◆ *Screwdrivers*
- ◆ *Sockets/spanners: 10–12mm*
- ◆ *Trolley jack and axle stands*
- ◆ *Wire brush*

Time: 2–3 hours
On your own? No

3. Try to carefully undo the brake pipe nut where it's attached to the flexi-hose. If the nut turns, make sure the pipe doesn't turn with it, as it will twist and eventually break off. Work the nut in and out and spray more penetrating fluid.

1. Make sure you can undo the 12mm banjo bolt that secures the brake flexi-hose to the brake caliper. Once it has been slackened and fluid leaks out, press the brake pedal and wedge it down with a length of wood against the driver's seat to prevent further fluid loss.

4. Once the brake pipe has been detached from the flexi-hose, use a flat-blade screwdriver to prise off the retaining clip that secures the pipework to the mount. This is a universal clip, so if it's corroded or breaks it can be replaced.

2. Spray lots of penetrating fluid over the other end of the brake flexi-hose where it's attached to the brake pipe. This will probably be heavily corroded, so clean the area with a wire brush and leave the penetrating fluid to soak in.

5. The old brake flexi-hose can now be detached from the brake caliper by fully undoing the banjo bolt, and then removed from the car. Wipe up any brake fluid that spills out as it is corrosive, especially on paintwork.

6. Check that the nut on the end of the brake pipe is clean. Wind the respective end of the new flexi-hose into the brake pipe by hand. Do not fully tighten it yet – the flexi-hose may become twisted.

7. Attach the other end of the brake flexi-hose to the caliper with a banjo bolt and two new copper washers. Do not fully tighten any of the fixings. Turn the steering from lock to lock and check the flexi-hose doesn't foul anything or become overstretched.

8. When you are satisfied that all flexi-hoses are correctly routed, tighten all fittings, refit the retaining clip from step 4 and bleed the brakes. Make sure the brake pedal is firm and there are no leaks from the connections for the flexi-hoses.

better handling

A good starting point for improving the handling of the MX-5 is to make sure the standard components that affect it are in good condition. The tyres can make a huge difference, so invest in a reputable brand before moving on to the suspension. Similarly, check the wheels are balanced and also check whether you have the right wheels fitted. Some aftermarket wheels may be too heavy and too large for the MX-5, resulting in excessive unsprung weight, which can result in scuttle shake and poor handling.

One of the best investments for improving the handling of the MX-5 is to have the tracking four-wheel aligned. This can make a massive difference to how the car drives, brakes and corners. The MX-5 suspension is fully adjustable at the front and rear, allowing for the camber and toe-in/out of the wheels to be set.

The 17in aftermarket alloy wheel fitted here weighs twice as much as the 14in standard wheel on the right. In this case, it had a negative effect on the car's handling.

The inner mounting bolts for the front and rear lower arms can be adjusted to alter the camber of the wheels.

NEW SPRINGS AND DAMPERS

The MX-5 uses upper and lower wishbones at all four corners with a vertically mounted coilover and front and rear anti-roll bars. It's a textbook design that works perfectly and has helped to create the car's reputation for having fantastic handling capabilities. For road use, this setup is brilliant, but it should be renewed with new springs and dampers to maintain the car's impeccable road-handling characteristics. There are also plenty of suspension specialists offering uprated springs and dampers, which can be of benefit if you wish to lower the ride height, reduce body roll and stiffen up the handling.

In theory, a full set of springs and dampers can be fitted in less than a day, but problems will always arise. The lower mounting bolt for the rear coilovers, for instance, can seize and require major surgery if its concealed captive nut becomes loose. Applying lots of penetrating fluid beforehand can often help here. In some cases, you can resort to using a hand-held blowtorch to apply heat to a seized fitting.

There's not a lot of room to extract the coilovers, particularly at the front, so extra help is essential, along with a selection of long metal bars for applying leverage. Professional tools also save time, such as a two-post ramp and a substantial spring compressor, but the work involved is well within the realms of a DIY job.

The following pages give several step-by-step guides, showing how to remove the front and rear coilovers, build up the new components and fit them on to the MX-5.

Removing the Front Coilovers

1. Spray over all the fittings that need to be undone using penetrating fluid, and clean off any dirt, including the anti-roll bar's drop link, the track rod end, lower mounting bolt for the coilover and the upper ball joint.

2. The upper ball joint that secures the upper wishbone to the upright needs to be detached. First extract the split pin that's fitted through the end of the ball joint's thread (it prevents the securing nut from moving).

> **TOOLBOX**
>
> ◆ **Blowtorch or oxyacetylene**
> ◆ **Breaker bar and ratchet**
> ◆ **Hammer**
> ◆ **Impact driver**
> ◆ **Long metal bars**
> ◆ **Paint for marking components**
> ◆ **Penetrating fluid**
> ◆ **Pry bars**
> ◆ **Screwdrivers**
> ◆ **Sockets/spanners: 10–18mm**
> ◆ **Spring compressor or clamps**
> ◆ **Two-post ramp or trolley jack and axle stands**
> ◆ **Vice grips**
> ◆ **Wire brush**

> **Time: 6–10 hours**
> **On your own? No**

3. Undo and remove the 17mm castle nut on the end of the upper ball joint. Make sure the ball joint's thread doesn't spin with the nut. Lever between the upper arm and upright if it does.

4. Separate the ball joint from the upright by hitting the side of the upright with a hammer to shock and release it. Do not damage the ball joint – it's pressed into the upper wishbone and cannot be renewed.

5. Detach the drop links from the anti-roll bar. Try to slacken the 14mm nut on the end of the drop link. If the thread spins, carefully grip the thread with an Allen key or vice grips.

8. Undo a 12mm bolt on the side of the coilover, which secures a mounting bracket for the ABS wire. Trace this wire inside the wheelarch and undo any more securing bolts to prevent it from being stretched when the coilover is removed.

6. If the 14mm nut on the end of the drop link cannot be undone, apply heat using a blowtorch or oxyacetylene, then undo the nut with an impact driver (grip the thread with vice grips).

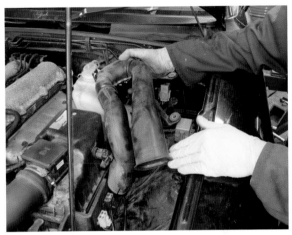

9. From inside the engine bay, look for the nuts that secure the top of each coilover. Part of the induction system will be obscuring the mounting nuts on the near side (left), so remove it by undoing a couple of 10mm bolts.

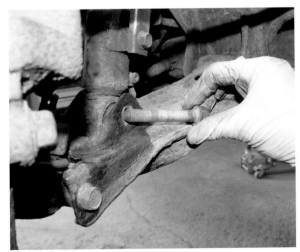

7. Undo the 17mm nut and bolt that secure the bottom of the coilover to the lower arm. Wind the bolt out and store aside for refitting later with the new suspension components.

10. Spray penetrating fluid over the two 14mm nuts that secure the top of each coilover, then carefully undo them. Wind the nuts in and out to clean the threads and reduce the risk of shearing the studs.

11. You are now ready to extract the front coilovers. Using two long pry bars or something similar, lever down on the upper wishbone with one of them and the lower arm with another. Apply more leverage on the lower arm.

12. Extract each front coilover up and through the upper wishbone, levering down on the lower arm for clearance. This is awkward, as the wheelarch gets in the way and there's not much room to manoeuvre with the lower arm in the way.

Removing the Rear Coilovers

1. The lower mounting bolt for each rear coilover is partly concealed, so it's worth spraying lots of penetrating fluid inside to ensure the bolt isn't seized inside the captive nut and the bush. Use a straw to help spray inside.

2. Fit an 18mm socket over the bottom mounting bolt and hit it with a hammer to help shock it and hopefully release it. This can also be done with a short extension bar to help shock the bolt.

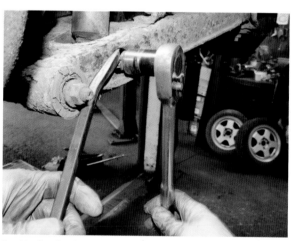

3. Undo the bottom mounting bolt. You will probably need to use a breaker bar to slacken it at first, then finish off with a ratchet. Lever the bolt out with a short pry bar once it has been fully undone.

4. Detach the drop link from the lower arm by undoing the 14mm nut and gripping the thread with an Allen key or vice grips. If the nut is seized, *see* the next step for further help.

5. If the drop link's thread spins with the 14mm nut and there seems to be no way of separating the two, you will have to resort to using heat, such as a blowtorch or oxyacetylene.

8. Use a short pry bar to release the bottom of the coilover from the lower arm. It sits inside the lower arm and will probably be surrounded with dirt and corrosion, making it difficult to separate.

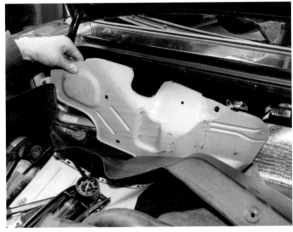

6. Look inside the boot and find the tops of the coilovers. Remove any carpeting and the metal panel shown here, which is secured with three 10mm bolts (only fitted on the near, or left, side of the boot).

9. Use a long pry bar or steel bar to lever down on the lower arm and manoeuvre the coilover out and to the side. Don't trap your fingers in the coils of the spring. If necessary, ask someone to help.

7. Spray penetrating fluid over the two 14mm nuts that secure the top of each coilover to the bodywork. Carefully undo them, winding the nuts in and out if they feel stiff to reduce the risk of shearing the studs.

10. Use a wire brush to clean inside the mounting point on the lower arm where the coilover sits. There will probably be lots of dirt and rust inside here, which should be removed before fitting the replacement coilover.

Fitting the New Springs and Dampers

1. It's important to mark the position of the upper and lower mounts to ensure they are the same when assembling the new coilovers. Use paint to make a mark and note how these parts should be fitted.

4. Once the nut has been removed from the top of the damper, the top plate and other parts can be carefully removed and the spring compressor or clamps slowly released. Place everything on a bench or the floor.

2. The old coilovers need to be dismantled to reuse the spring rubbers, bump stops, dust covers and top mount components. Use a spring compressor or spring clamps to safely compress the spring and take any tension off the upper mount.

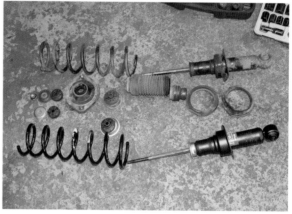

5. Remove all of the parts that make up the coilover and carefully arrange them in the order they are fitted. Lay the new damper and coil spring alongside. Renew any components that appear worn or damaged.

3. With the spring compressed, use an impact driver to undo the top nut. There may be one locking nut fitted or two nuts (undo each one in turn). Check the thread doesn't spin when undoing the nut(s).

6. Carefully compress the new spring with clamps or a spring compressor. There may be a label or some indication to show which way up it should be fitted. If not, see how it should be fitted into the damper.

7. Fit the new damper and refit the spring rubbers, bump stop, dust cover and upper mounting parts. New parts may be supplied with your damper, such as the upper rubber bushes and top plates.

8. Carefully tighten the top nut to the recommended torque setting (if supplied). You may need to grip the thread with an Allen key to prevent it from spinning. The end of the thread shown here has two flats to grip.

Fitting the New Coilovers

1. Before fitting each newly assembled coilover, double-check that the two studs at the top are correctly aligned with the mounting hole at the bottom. On the front coilovers there's also a thread for the ABS wire's securing bracket.

2. The rear coilovers are easier to fit than the fronts. Use a long pry bar or steel bar to lever down on the lower arm, then manoeuvre the coilover up and into the turret in the bodywork and into the lower arm.

3. Once you have managed to get a rear coilover into position, make sure the two top studs are poking through the bodywork, then fit the 14mm nuts that go on the end of them. Don't fully tighten them yet.

4. Use a screwdriver to line up the hole in the rear lower arm with the hole in the bottom of the coilover. You may need to lever down on the bottom arm if the coilover gets stuck inside its mounting location.

5. Fit the 18mm bolt through the rear lower arm and the coilover. Do not fully tighten it until the car is back on to its wheels; all other fittings (top 14mm nuts and drop links) can be fully tightened.

8. Reposition the upper arm's ball joint into the upright, then refit the castle nut and split pin. If the ball joint spins with the nut, lever between the end of the upper arm and the upright to prevent it from moving.

6. To fit the front coilovers, pull down on the upper wishbone and feed the coilover through from the top. Ask someone to pull or lever down on the lower arm to help feed the bottom of the coilover into position.

9. Refit the 17mm nut and bolt that secure the bottom of the coilover – fully tighten them when the car is back on its wheels. Refit the drop link and the securing bracket for the ABS wire.

7. Once the front coilover is in position and the two threads at the top have been fed through the respective holes in the turret, fit the two 14mm nuts by hand, but do not fully tighten them yet.

10. Hand tighten the two 14mm nuts that secure the top of the coilover (do not over-tighten them). Refit the road wheels, test drive the car, then check that all fittings at the front and rear are secure.

UPRATED SUSPENSION BUSHES

If you're keen to improve the handling of your MX-5, then one of cheapest starting points is to fit some uprated suspension bushes. The benefits can include a firmer ride quality with more positive and precise steering, but it's best to fit only a few uprated bushes at a time to help assess whether there are any benefits. It's also worth looking into the short scale hardness of the bushes you choose. Some can be tailored to be as soft as OE bushes, whereas others may be too harsh.

Most polyurethane suspension bush manufacturers promise their products are fit and forget. Unlike rubber suspension bushes that can wear, polyurethane doesn't appear to wear out under normal road use.

There are a number of potential disadvantages to fitting polyurethane suspension bushes, though. The problems can start when you try to remove the old suspension components that you intend to re-bush – fixings can seize or shear off. And when you try to remove some of the old bushes, you may need to use a hydraulic press or even resort to cutting or burning them out.

TOOLBOX

- ◆ **Blowtorch or oxyacetylene**
- ◆ **Bucket of water**
- ◆ **Copper grease**
- ◆ **Drifts**
- ◆ **Gloves and goggles**
- ◆ **Hacksaw**
- ◆ **Hammers**
- ◆ **Hydraulic press**
- ◆ **Penetrating fluid**
- ◆ **Plastic mallet**
- ◆ **Pry bars**
- ◆ **Screwdrivers**
- ◆ **Spanners/sockets: 12–21mm**
- ◆ **Vice**

Time: 8–24 hours
On your own? No

Front Upper Wishbone

1. The front upper wishbones can be removed along with the upright/hub and the brake. First, spray penetrating fluid over all nuts and bolts and try to free off the long inner bolt for the wishbone using 20mm and 21mm spanners.

2. Remove the brake caliper by undoing its 14mm and 17mm bolts, and suspend it to avoid overstretching the flexi-hose. Remove the caliper carrier (two 14mm bolts) followed by the brake disc – removing these two parts creates more space.

3. Undo the nut and bolt that secures the bottom of the coilover to the lower arm. This should be a 17mm head for both fittings. It may have seized, so apply lots of penetrating fluid first and throughout undoing it.

4. The lower ball joint will be removed with the upper wishbone and hub/upright, so undo the 17mm bolt, which secures the ball joint into the lower arm (located below the lower coilover mount). This is easier than separating the ball joint.

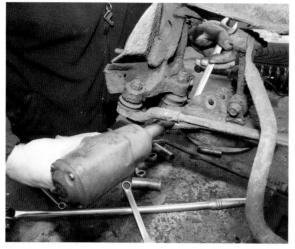

5. Remove the pinch bolt for the lower ball joint. This also keeps it secured to the lower arm. The pinch bolt should have a 17mm head and a 14mm nut and will probably need to be wound or drifted out.

8. You're now ready to remove the long bolt that was slackened in step 1 and, in turn, remove the upper wishbone and hub/upright together. The upper ball joint must be carefully separated – damage it and you'll need to buy a new arm.

Front Lower Wishbone

6. Separate the track rod end on the steering rack from where it's secured to the steering arm on the hub/upright. First remove a split pin, then undo a 17mm nut and hit the side of the steering arm to release it.

1. Detach the drop link from the lower arm, secured with a 14mm nut and bolt, or a 14mm nut with an Allen key hole in the end of the drop link's thread. The latter fixing may need heat to undo.

7. If your MX-5 has ABS, the wiring to the ABS sensor on the hub will need to be disconnected (usually the sensor cannot be removed from the hub). Undo all mounting points for the wiring and disconnect it inside the engine bay.

2. The lower arm is secured to the MX-5's front subframe in two places with 17mm nuts and bolts. Undo the 17mm nuts and try to free off the bolts so they can be wound out of the bushes.

3. The inner mounting bolts can be quite awkward to access and wind out. As you unwind them, you may need to poke a screwdriver through the bush to help push the bolt out. The bolt can corrode inside the bush.

2. Undo the lower mounting for the rear anti-roll bar's drop links. This may be a 14mm nut and bolt, or a 14mm nut with an Allen key hole in the thread (*see* the next step if this is the case).

4. Once the two inner mounting bolts have been removed, the entire front lower arm can also be removed from the MX-5. Check its condition, looking for signs of excessive corrosion that may mean it needs replacing.

3. If the drop links are only secured with a 14mm nut and no bolt, you may need to apply some heat to be able to undo the nut. The drop link's thread will probably spin and the Allen key hole is weak.

Rear Anti-Roll Bar

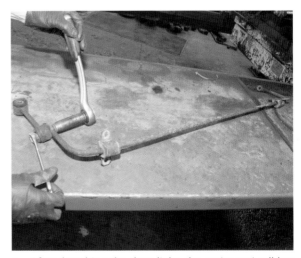

1. The bushes for the rear anti-roll bar drop links and mounts can be replaced with polyurethane. Undo the 14mm nuts for the D-bush mounts. These will probably be corroded, so apply plenty of penetrating fluid.

4. After detaching the drop links, the entire anti-roll bar can be removed from the MX-5. The drop links can then be removed from the ends of the anti-roll bar with more room to work on them.

Rear Upper Wishbone

1. The rear brakes need to be removed to create a little more space, so undo the 14mm caliper carrier bolts and prise off the entire carrier and brake caliper together. Suspend them aside and remove the brake disc.

2. Undo the 14mm nut and bolt that hold the outer part of the upper wishbone to the top of the upright. Extract the bolt and ease the two components apart. The bush inside the top of the upright can be renewed.

3. The inner part of the upper wishbone is secured in two places with a 17mm nut and 14mm bolt. Access is a little awkward and these fittings will be very tight. There are holes in the rear subframe to fit socket extensions.

4. Once the two inner bolts have been undone and removed, the upper arm can then be removed from the MX-5 and inspected for corrosion and damage. You may need to waggle it up and down to help release it.

Rear Lower Wishbone

1. Undo the 18mm bottom coilover mounting bolt and wind it out. This is fitted into a captive nut, so spray penetrating fluid into it to help prevent the captive nut from shearing off (it's prone to corrosion).

2. The lower wishbone is secured to two points on the rear subframe with 17mm bolts and 14mm nuts. Remove the nuts, then drift and wind out the bolts to release the lower wishbone from these two mounting points.

3. Undo the 17mm nut on the end of the long 21mm bolt that holds the outer part of the lower wishbone to the upright. If the bolt is seized, the entire hub and upright will need to be removed to drift it out.

2. Cut off any exposed parts of the old bushes using a hacksaw. In some cases this will help to drift or press out the old bush, but it also helps to see what needs to be removed.

4. The lower wishbone can now be removed, but if the outer bolt is seized, undo the hub nut, then try to release the hub/upright with the lower wishbone attached. If this fails, detach the driveshaft at the diff.

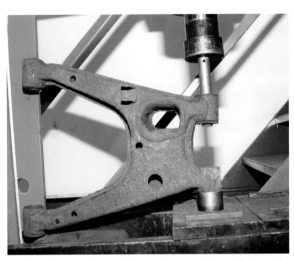

3. Pressing out the old bushes is one of the safest methods of removing them. Do not use a vice as it may break. After pressing out a bush, clean inside the area where it was fitted, making sure there are no remains.

Inspection and Bush Removal

1. Check the condition of all the suspension components you intend to renew with uprated bushes. As the photograph shows, here the front upper wishbone on the right has a bent inner mount, so it cannot be reused.

4. If a bush cannot be removed, the last resort is to burn it out. Only do this outside as the fumes are toxic, and wear goggles, a mask and gloves. Have a bucket of water nearby and do not touch any of the suspension components afterwards.

Fitting New Bushes

1. Most polyurethane bushes do not require a hydraulic press to fit them. Apply some copper grease around the outer surfaces of the bush. This helps with fitting, but also reduces the risk of the bushes squeaking when fitted.

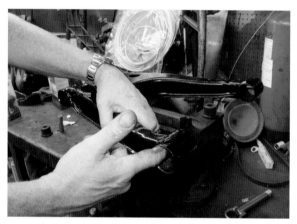

2. Make sure the housings where the new bushes will be fitted are clean and not damaged. Apply a smear of copper grease inside them to help with fitting the bushes and reducing any unwanted suspension squeaks.

3. The new bushes will probably consist of two polyurethane halves and a steel insert. Fit one half in position, followed by the insert. You may need to use a vice to squeeze the second half into position.

4. It may be easier to fit both halves of the polyurethane bush, then fit the steel insert at the end. Again, you may need to use a vice to squeeze it into position. A plastic mallet can also help.

BANDED STEEL WHEELS

Steel wheels are back in fashion and the ones to have if you like a traditional look. Wider steel wheels can look awesome on an MX-5 and this modification involves welding a steel band to increase the width across the wheel, which allows an equally wider tyre to be fitted. However, this isn't something that can be done at home with a MIG welder and tape measure. The following photographs show how Alonze Custom Fabrication (www.alonzecustom. co.uk) dismantle a steel wheel and weld a band of steel to it using their own jigs and equipment for optimum accuracy.

Rim Removal

1. Alonze Custom Fabrication starts the banding conversion by dot punching the point on the inside of the wheel that is next to the hole for the tyre valve. This ensures the rim is fitted in the same position after the band.

4. After cutting a line all the way round the outer rim, it can be parted from the wheel. It needs a little persuasion with a hammer, but providing the cut is sufficiently deep, the outer rim will fall off.

2. The wheel is secured in a jig that half resembles a wheel balancing machine, but with an angle grinder and cutting disc attached. A specially made centre boss is required to secure the wheel's centre bore in position.

5. Here's the wheel and the outer rim that has been cut off. A 3mm thick steel band will be welded between the outer rim and the wheel to widen the wheel and allow wider tyres to be fitted.

3. As the wheel is slowly turned on the jig via an electric motor, the angle grinder is switched on and its cutting disc slices through the first skin of the outer rim of the wheel. It won't cut all the way through the steel wheel.

6. Before the new steel band is fitted, the areas of the wheel and rim where they will be welded need to be cleaned. This is where working with a new steel wheel is better, but old wheels can be cleaned up.

Making a Band

1. Making the required band starts with a large sheet of 3mm-thick steel. A section is cut off using an electric powered guillotine. It slices through the steel like butter, making a clean cut.

2. The length of flat steel needs to have bevelled edges to make it easier to weld to the wheel. A bevelling machine can do this and it's more accurate and a lot quicker than trying to do this by hand.

3. The length of flat steel is run through an industrial-sized mangle to turn it into a band. This takes several passes, gradually bending the length of flat steel into shape. The same equipment can be used to make cylinders.

4. The diameter of the band isn't too important at this stage, as it can be adjusted to fit around the wheel. Any excess will be trimmed off later, so providing it forms a band, that's all that matters for now.

Welding the Rim and Band

1. The first stage in welding the band in position is to TIG weld it to the outer rim. Several spot welds are added between the rim and band to initially position it, and a straight edge is used to check the two are evenly fitted.

2. The ends of the band overlap, so the excess has to be cut off. A diagonal cut is made using an angle grinder, which will be seam welded later. For now, the band remains tack welded to the outer rim.

3. With the outer rim and band tack welded together using a TIG welder, it's now time to fit the band over the wheel. This will help to achieve the correct shape for the band and enable it and the outer rim to be seam welded together.

4. The band and outer rim are positioned over the wheel and hammered into positon using a plastic mallet. The outer rim and band will be separated from the wheel once they have been seam welded together.

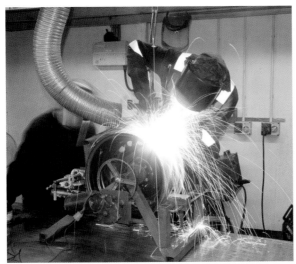

5. With the wheel secured in the jig and rotating at a constant speed, the outer rim and band are seam welded together. While one person MIG welds, another person checks it and adjusts the speed of the rotating wheel.

6. After seam welding the outer rim and band together, they are removed from the wheel to allow the join in the band to be welded. This diagonal cut was made in step 2. A seam weld is essential here for an airtight seal.

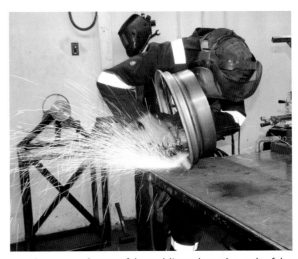

7. The exposed areas of the welding where the ends of the band are joined and where the outer rim joins the band are tidied up. A neat finish is essential here and it needs to be airtight, so it will be tested later.

8. The exposed area of the band is cleaned on a sanding drum using a P60-grit paper. The clean metal surface and the rest of the wheel will need to be painted soon after to prevent them from rusting.

Final Welding

1. With the outer rim and band seam welded together, all that remains is to fit them on to the wheel, check they are correctly aligned, then weld everything together. The mallet is used once more to fit the band over the wheel.

3. The band and wheel are tack welded at this stage, measuring after each weld to ensure the wheel rotates true. This is difficult with wheels that are often slightly out of true to start with.

2. Before the band and outer rim can be welded on to the wheel, they must be correctly aligned, so they're fitted on the jig and turned to ensure they rotate true. Measurements are taken along the outer rim and across the width of the wheel.

4. Confident the band is correctly located and tack welded to the wheel, the operator transfers these parts to the welding jig, where they are seam welded together. The wheel is rotated throughout welding.

Leak Testing

Once the banded wheel has been welded and allowed to cool, a tyre valve is inserted the wrong way round, then a hydraulic press is used to conduct a leak test. Using thick sheets of rubber and wood, the banded wheel is sandwiched in position and air is fed into the sealed area of the rim of the wheel. This is the opposite way round to how air will be contained by the tyre, but is sufficient to trace any leaks, especially using the same test liquids as used by gas plumbers.

bodywork and hood

ROTTEN BODYWORK

The steel-bodied MX-5 can corrode, especially in wet countries where salt is spread on the roads during winter. The most common area of corrosion is the sill that runs between the front and rear wheels. The area close to the rear wheels is particularly well-known for rotting through and failing the MOT test. Fortunately, repair panels and complete sill panels are available.

Other areas that corrode include the wheelarches and the battery box in the boot. However, the most terminal corrosion that can be found is inside the chassis legs. These areas can be inspected from underneath the MX-5 but can be difficult to repair without dismantling a large proportion of the car.

A large part of this chapter deals with preserving the MX-5's bodywork, but also covers rust repairs and how to weld in new metal. The following steps show how to cut out a section of corrosion and make a patch.

TOOLBOX

- ◆ *Angle grinder*
- ◆ *Body filler*
- ◆ *Fire extinguisher*
- ◆ *MIG welder*
- ◆ *Safety goggles*
- ◆ *Tin snips*
- ◆ *Welding mask and gloves*
- ◆ *Wet and dry paper (P80–P800 grit)*

Time: 1–2 hours
On your own? Yes

Patch Repairs

1. If a small area on a wheelarch, for example, has corroded, it may be easier to cut out the rot and weld in a patch. Start with an angle grinder and cutting disc to remove the rotten metalwork.

2. Cut out a clean piece of sheet steel to fit inside the hole. The piece of metal shown here extends beyond the arch, but it will be trimmed in situ after it has been welded in position.

3. Disconnect the battery and make sure you have a fire extinguisher to hand. Tack weld the new patch into position, making sure it remains flush with the rest of the wheelarch.

4. Trim off any excess sheet metal if required – this will make it easier to shape the edge of the patch against the rest of the wheelarch. Seam weld all the way around the patch.

5. Tidy up the weld with an angle grinder to achieve a smooth finish that's flush with the rest of the wheelarch. You may need to return to welding if you spot any holes or gaps.

6. Protect the clean metal with paint, then blend it into the bodywork with a skim of filler and rub it down with wet and dry paper – repeat until you achieve a smooth finish.

RUSTPROOFING

Rust has still got to be the number one enemy of the MX-5, especially in the UK, where the winter road salt turns the sills and chassis legs into crumbling piles of iron oxide.

The market is awash with experts and opinions concerning the best products and the best methods for rustproofing a car such as the MX-5. There's no escaping the fact that a thorough rustproofing job is going to take a long weekend, or several evenings.

However, rustproofing should also be an ongoing process, a bit like painting the Forth Road Bridge – once you've finished, it's time to start again.

Rust, as it's commonly known, is the chemical conversion of iron to iron oxide. It requires oxygen and water to complete the process, which are present in abundance in most climates. Materials made from iron and steel can easily turn to iron oxide for a number of reasons. First, iron oxide is iron's natural form when it is extracted from the ground as iron ore, so it has a tendency to return to this state. Second, when iron ore is made into iron or steel, the resulting material contains energy, which is similar to the voltage in a battery. Add water to the equation and that energy can be released, resulting in oxidation.

The deadly mix of water, energy and metal becomes even more problematic when moisture becomes trapped between panels, especially if those panels are of differing grades of steel. The effect is similar to a battery, resulting in accelerated corrosion. This problem can also arise with rusty bolts and the surrounding panelwork.

Other materials can oxidize in a similar manner. Aluminium, for instance, can oxidize and become opaque – a common problem on the MX-5's aluminium bonnet. Copper, such as in brake pipes, turns green when it oxidizes.

The preparation involved prior to applying rust prevention products is important. Remove as many panels as possible to help access the areas of the car that need to be rust protected. Clean the bodywork, removing flaky paint, rust and other materials that can prevent paint, underseal, wax and other products from sticking to the surface.

Rustproofing Tools

Different sizes of scrapers help to remove underseal, flaky paint and rust. Small and large steel wire brushes are useful

Popular rustproofing tools include a selection of scrapers, safety goggles, gloves, spray bottles and a few plugs or bungs.

for scrubbing, whilst wire brush wheels, which are attached to a drill or angle grinder, are labour saving. Old spray bottles are useful for spraying warmed-up wax into doors, but don't expect the spray mechanism to last too long before the wax blocks it up.

If you need to drill some holes into sills and chassis sections to spray wax into them, the holes should be protected with plugs. These are available from most rustproofing specialists.

Don't forget to protect yourself when rustproofing. Wear safety goggles, gloves and a breathing mask before scraping off old underseal and applying rust protection.

Rust Killers

There are lots of products available that promise to convert rust back to metal and stop rust spreading. Many have received mixed reviews as to their effectiveness, but there are some useful products available that can genuinely help to fight corrosion. Don't expect any rust cure product to be able to transform a crumbly panel that's full of holes back into a shiny piece of metal: this is impossible to achieve. Similarly, don't expect simply to paint a product on to a dirty, rusty surface and see it transform into new steel. A little elbow grease is essential first and a rusty surface needs to be clear of flaky paint and contaminants before applying any product.

Most rust cures are intended to stop rust spreading. Hammerite's Kurust, for instance, is a paint-on solution that converts rusty metal to a clean surface in fifteen minutes. Similarly, its Rust Beater can be painted onto rusty metal and acts as a primer and undercoat. Rustbuster provides an interesting explanation of how its Fe-123 molecular rust converter works when applied to a clean but rusty surface, stating 'This converter actually uses natural substances bound in a latex film to physically change the nature of the steel's surface from iron oxide to iron tannate. This can then be painted with Rustbuster Epoxy-Mastic 121.'

TOOLBOX

- Breathing mask
- Cloths and towels
- Masking tape
- Metal paint
- Penetrating fluid
- Rustproofing equipment and wax
- Safety goggles
- Spanners/sockets: 14mm
- Torch
- Trim tools
- Underseal
- White spirit
- Wire brush

Time: 8–16 hours
On your own? Yes

Rustproofing – Golden Rules

- Rustproofing a car can be a disastrous exercise if you get it wrong. For instance, hot weather can warm up wax, resulting in it leaking out of door and sill drain holes. Don't be alarmed if your car drips a brown/yellow liquid. Just remember to apply more wax when the weather isn't so hot.
- Most waxes can be washed off, so don't use them on exposed wheelarches or outer sills, where road muck and rainwater can rinse it away. Underseal is more suitable in these areas, although special weatherproof wax is available.

◆ Wax is flammable, so don't spray it into an area that needs welding or grinding as it will set on fire and could be difficult to extinguish. Also, avoid spraying wax over hot components (such as the exhaust).

◆ Wax can be difficult to apply in a cold climate as it becomes hard and will block spray equipment. Stand the wax container in a bucket or jug of hot water to warm it up and keep warming it up when applying it.

◆ If the inside of a sill isn't fully coated in wax, moisture will settle in any exposed areas, resulting in a greater concentration of corrosion. And don't forget that rust-proofing cannot fix a rotten panel. Wax and underseal can only slow down the corrosion process, at best. Rust can spread, so remove or stop it – don't simply rustproof over it.

The best solution for this mounting bracket in an MX-5's engine bay is to remove it and fit a new one.

◆ Avoid blocking drain holes with wax or underseal. They are designed to allow water to drain through the chassis, doors and body. Blocking them will result in water filling up inside, which leads to more corrosion.

◆ Take your time when rustproofing. Preparation is key, so make sure the area you want to rustproof is clean and any surrounding surfaces are protected. There's no point in slapping some underseal on and hoping it will stick to the underside of a rusty and dirty MX-5.

Sills and Cross-Members

1. A wax-based rustproofing product can be injected inside the sills and cross-members. If you are applying this on a cold day, warm up the solution in a bucket of warm water to help reduce the risk of it clogging up the spray equipment.

2. The MX-5's seats should be removed to allow the cross-members to be inspected. Slide each seat fully forwards to undo the two 14mm bolts at the rear, then fully back to undo the two front mounting bolts.

3. Use a set of plastic trim tools to lever up the trim panel across the top of the sill. This should be clipped into position, but it may also be secured with some screws. It needs to be removed before you can lift up the carpet.

4. Peel back the carpet to check the condition of the floors. Old soundproofing material may be underneath. If it's wet, remove it to dry it out, or discard it – *see* Chapter 10 for a soundproofing guide.

5. The biggest potential rust problem for the MX-5 is the sills, so use a torch to look inside to see if corrosion has set in. The photograph here shows a magnetic pickup tool with a light on the end that can be shone inside the sill.

8. Wipe away any residue with a cloth soaked in a little white spirit. The last job is to thoroughly clean the spray equipment with white spirit or warm water to ensure it can be used again in the future.

Wheelarches

6. Spray a rustproofing wax inside the sills and try to apply an even coating. This is difficult, despite there being several holes, but an even coating is essential to ensure that any exposed metal doesn't become more prone to corrosion.

1. Raise a corner of the MX-5 and support with an axle stand. Using a selection of trim tools and screwdrivers, remove all the fixings for the inner arch trim. Some of these fixings will probably break and will need replacing.

7. The insides of the cross-members and box sections that form the floor can be coated in a rustproofing wax as well. You can also spray it through any holes in the A-post, around the door hinges and check strap.

2. Once all of the inner wheelarch panels have been removed, use a wire brush to remove all of the dirt and corrosion on the metalwork of the arch. Any areas that you intend to rustproof must be clean.

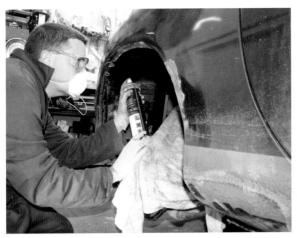

3. Place a large unwanted towel over the brakes and suspension components. Apply a coat of underseal and leave it for the recommended amount of time before applying another coat (repeat again if necessary).

1. Use a wire brush to scrape off any old underseal, rust and dirt from the underside of the car. The chassis legs, sills and floors need to be protected, as they are often peppered with road dirt, salt and water.

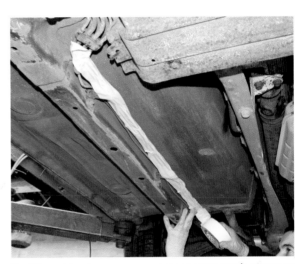

4. Leave the underseal to dry for at least 24 hours before refitting the trim panels inside the wheelarch. If any of the fittings broke off, *see* the separate instructions on repairing a sheared fitting below.

Rustproofing the Underside

Underseal is an effective form of protection for the external areas of a car you rarely need to touch, such as the underneath and inside the wheelarches. Its tar-like qualities means it remains flexible for several years and provides protection to panels and components (such as axle casings) that may occasionally move or flex. It's also useful for soundproofing.

There are various thicknesses of underseal, which dictate how they can be applied. The really thick stuff is supplied in a tin and needs to be applied with a brush. This is only useful for surfaces that are easy to access, however. If you want to thoroughly coat a chassis cross-member, for instance, use a spray-on underseal. Thin underseal can be applied using an aerosol can, but the best coverage is achieved using air-fed equipment and disposable underseal canisters.

Underseal isn't a cure for corrosion. If a panel has already rotted, applying a coat of underseal may result in the rust accelerating, especially if moisture is trapped inside. Make sure any panels you intend to underseal are clean and free of corrosion.

2. Fit masking tape over any components you do not want to cover with underseal. Even if you are applying the underseal with a brush, it can still escape onto brake pipes and fuel lines.

3. If you are applying underseal with an aerosol or air-fed equipment, wear a suitable breathing mask and googles. Apply a thin coat, leave it to dry for the recommended time, then apply another coat.

Battery Box Protection

1. The battery box area in the boot and the same storage area on the opposite side are prone to collecting water, which leads to corrosion. Regular inspection, drying and cleaning are essential. If rust has formed, remove it with a wire brush.

There's nothing quite like a sheared nut or bolt to send the spanners flying. A straightforward job can turn into an entire evening spent drilling and tapping just because a bolt becomes decapitated. Most of us have experienced this and been left swearing at a small inanimate object whose rusty thread or objection to being undone is halting progress.

Seized fixings are often inevitable, especially on older MX-5s that have been subjected to road salt and other equally corrosive substances. It's a potential problem on all MX-5s, however, especially the plastic fixings, where they become brittle and perish. The trick is to know how to resolve such problems before they happen. Avoid losing your temper when undoing fixings that are awkward or seized. Think around the problem before you arm yourself with an angle grinder, cut up the entire car and weigh it in for scrap.

Penetrating fluid is one of the best remedies for a seized fixing. Apply lots to the thread and leave it to soak in for several hours. If you can submerge the fixing, then leave it overnight in a bowl of penetrating fluid, petrol, paraffin or white spirit (just one of them).

2. Any exposed metal in the battery box area should be protected with a suitable paint. The entire area can be further protected with a rubberized paint, such as Frost's Liquid Wrap (also known as ElastiWrap).

Always clean the flats of a bolt head or nut before undoing it. This will help to achieve a secure grip for a socket or spanner and reduce the risk of slipping and damaging the flats. Use a steel wire brush to clean the flats, but avoid the threads.

3. Waterproofing the battery box may be the best solution, especially if it seems impossible to fix the cause of the leak. Adding drain holes will also help here, along with regular inspections to ensure the area remains dry.

Penetrating fluid can make the difference between shearing a bolt and successfully slackening it.

Heat is often the only solution to undoing a seized nut or bolt, especially ones for the suspension.

If the exposed thread of a bolt or stud looks rusty or damaged, try cleaning it up first with a thread file. Do not use a steel wire brush as it will damage the threads. If you don't have a thread file, try using a strong sewing needle or the edge of a three-sided needle file.

Hit the bolt head or the side of the nut with a hammer to help release it. The impact of the hammer sometimes moves it enough to be able to loosen it. Also, fit a socket on to the nut or bolt and hammer it on to ensure a tight fit.

If you manage to slacken a tough nut or bolt, don't be tempted to continue undoing it. Instead, work it back and forth and spray lots of penetrating fluid over it. This will clean the thread and reduce the risk of snapping the stud.

Applying heat to a seized nut or bolt allows the metal to expand, often making it easier to undo. For small fittings, a pocket-sized gas torch or hand-held blowtorch should be sufficient. Larger nuts and bolts, such as track rod end nuts, may need an oxyacetylene-fed blowtorch.

If you can't get enough leverage on a spanner, try using two. This works best with combination spanners that have a ring at one end and are open-ended at the other. Fit the ring end of one onto the nut or bolt, then attach the second spanner on to the end of the first to achieve more leverage.

If the flats on a nut or bolt become rounded and a socket or spanner slips when undoing it, try using a slightly smaller socket. You'll probably need to hammer it on to the nut or bolt. Try different sets of metric and AF sockets and spanners, including six-sided and twelve-sided. Some of these may have a better grip. Most sizes are interchangeable (14mm is similar to 9⁄16in AF).

Filing new flats onto a rounded nut or bolt can sometimes help to undo it. This isn't as easy as it sounds because the new flats need to be symmetrical. You'll need to use a smaller socket or spanner to undo the nut or bolt. If successful, discard it afterwards.

If the cross or slot in the head of a screw has become damaged, there are a number of solutions to removing it. If the head is raised, file a couple of flats, then use a pair of mole grips to remove it.

Plastic or inset screws where the sides of the head cannot be filed will need to be drilled out. This can be time-consuming. Start with a small drill bit and apply penetrating fluid to avoid overheating any metal.

If a seized nut cannot be removed, you can either remove the stud it's attached to and fit a new one, or cut the nut off. If you resort to the latter and want to preserve the thread, use a junior hacksaw to carefully cut along the walls of the nut. Cut down two opposite sides of the nut to release it.

Large nuts and bolts can sometimes be effectively slackened using a chisel. Position the end of the chisel against one of the flats of the nut or bolt on a 45-degree angle (towards the direction of slackening). Hit the top of the chisel's handle with a hammer to try to slacken the nut or bolt.

Some fixings can be drilled out, such as a plastic plug for trim, a clevis pin or a steel retaining screw for a disc brake. This will involve fitting a new plug or screw, and may also involve repairing the thread it fits into.

Brake pipe nuts can often be very difficult to undo and usually round off. If you're renewing a pipe, try cutting the brake pipe near the offending nut, then use a socket or ring spanner to undo it – this will provide a better grip than an open-ended spanner if the pipe wasn't cut.

One of the most satisfying solutions to a seized nut or bolt is to grind it off. Cover any areas such as upholstery and

The head of plastic trim screws can often round off, so the best answer is to drill them out.

glass to protect them from grinding sparks. Always wear goggles, gloves and a long-sleeved top to protect your skin and eyes.

So, once you've managed to undo a stubborn fixing, you may find you have even more repairs to attend to. If that's the case, then the next few pages outline a few solutions.

Rivet Nut Repairs

1. If a fixing such as a captive nut or threaded hole has been stripped or the remains of a bolt are left inside it, then one method of fixing it is to fit a rivet nut. Start by drilling a suitable hole to fit the rivet nut.

2. The rivet nut needs to be a tight fit when it's slotted into the hole to ensure it can be compressed and will grip itself in position. This allows a bolt to be threaded into it with little risk of the rivet nut turning.

3. There are a variety of rivet nut tools, all of which compress the rivet nut when it has been fitted into a hole in a panel. Squashing the rivet nut can be hard work, requiring the use of extra tools, such as a spanner.

4. The photograph here shows three rivet nuts fitted inside a rear wheelarch of a Mk2 MX-5. The trim panels can now be refitted and secured with suitable bolts threaded into the rivet nuts.

SWAPPING A HOOD AND FRAME

If the hood on an MX-5 is damaged beyond repair, there are usually two solutions. The first is to renew the hood fabric, which involves removing it from the hood frame – this is shown in detail later in this chapter. The second involves fitting a complete hood and frame from another MX-5. Thankfully, the hood and frame from the Mk1 and Mk2 are interchangeable, although the Mk1 has a plastic rear screen and the later Mk2 has glass. Some of the trim down the B-posts is slightly different, but the fixings are the same.

TOOLBOX

◆ *Spanners/sockets: 10, 12mm*
◆ *Torx bits: T40*
◆ *Trim tools*

Time: 1–2 hours
On your own? Yes

The MX-5's hood is secured to the vehicle in two areas. Along the back of the rear parcel shelf, there is a series of 10mm nuts, which clamp three metal braces in place to secure the back of the hood in position. Down the sides of the B-posts there are three 12mm bolts. This all sounds very straightforward, but the hood frame is bulky and awkward to remove, although it is usually possible to remove it on your own.

After fitting a replacement hood frame and hood, put the hood up and try to expose it to direct sunlight to allow the fabric to stretch.

3. The B-post trim needs to be removed in order to access the mounting bolts for the hood framework. First remove the side mounting points for the hardtop, which are each secured with a couple of Torx T40 bolts.

1. The back of the hood is secured to the bodywork with a series of 10mm nuts, most of which can be accessed from inside the car when the hood is up. These nuts secure three metal brace bars that clamp the back of the hood in position.

4. After removing a piece of rubber trim on the top of the B-post, and the door seal down the side of the B-post, the plastic trim that's secured to the inside of the B-post can be unclipped and removed.

2. If a windbreak is fitted, remove it for better access. It's usually secured with a couple of crosshead screws at each end, which are a little fiddly to undo due to a lack of space.

5. Three 12mm bolts for the hood frame are now visible through holes inside the B-post. These are relatively easy to undo, but fiddly to extract as they can easily fall down inside the B-post.

6. If the old hood has a glass screen, there's a micro-switch that needs to be removed, which is a safety measure to ensure the heated screen cannot be switched on when the hood is down.

2. Keep the hood folded out and refit the three metal brace bars at the rear of the hood. All the mounting studs should line up correctly, so refit all of the 10mm nuts.

7. After detaching the connector plug for the heated rear screen, the hood can be folded down and lifted up and off the car. This is a little awkward on your own, but possible, releasing one side at a time before lifting the entire hood away.

3. Progressively refit the 12mm mounting bolts down the sides of the B-posts, raising and lowering the hood to manoeuvre it into position and line up all six mounting points.

Fitting the Replacement Hood and Frame

1. Position the hood flat on to the back of the car, then fold it out and attach it across the top of the windscreen to check it fits down the B-posts. This can be awkward to do and you may think the mounting points don't line up at this stage.

4. The new hood may be tight to fit, but try to stretch it out and expose it to sunlight. It may need leaving up for a few days. If it's a second-hand hood, clean and protect it.

FITTING A NEW HOOD

The vinyl hood on the MX-5 Mk1 and Mk2 can begin to shrink and split over time, but all is not lost because new hoods are available.

Many hoods are supplied with a glass rear screen, which is an ideal upgrade from the plastic screen found on the Mk1. All MX-5s from 1991 have the wiring installed for the heated rear window.

The work involved in removing the old hood looks quite barbaric, especially if you study the following pictures, which were completed with Peter Jones from MazMania (www.mazmania.co.uk). The best approach is to avoid being too sympathetic towards your old hood, especially if it's going to be discarded. Simply slice through it with a sharp knife to remove it quickly. There are also several fittings to undo, which help you to understand the framework and how the hood is secured to the car. In brief, the back of the hood is secured to the bodywork; elsewhere, it's secured to the hood frame.

Renewing the hood is a good opportunity to check the drain holes and rustproof the framework, so take your time.

> *Time: 3–6 hours*
> *On your own? Yes*

TOOLBOX

- ◆ *Aerosol paint*
- ◆ *Cable ties*
- ◆ *¼in ratchet with 10mm socket*
- ◆ *Electric drill and 4mm drill bit*
- ◆ *Pop-rivet gun*
- ◆ *Screwdriver*
- ◆ *Sharp knife*
- ◆ *Thin metal rod*
- ◆ *Trim tool*
- ◆ *Wire brush*

Removing the Old Hood

1. Peter Jones confidently slices through an old hood, taking around ten minutes to remove the majority of it. Starting at the rear, cut out the rear screen so you can remove it, detaching any wiring for the heater elements.

2. Cut along the front of the hood, just before the header rail section and down the sides, above the door glass. You won't be able to remove the hood as it's secured to the framework.

3. Use a trim tool to lever open the retaining strips holding the hood to the frame (listing bow). Glass-screened hoods are only fitted to the front listing bow, plastic-screened hoods are attached to all three listing bows.

4. The hood that covers the rear and top can now be removed from the car and discarded. The framework is now exposed and you may discover some corrosion that should be treated by cleaning it off and painting the frame.

5. Use the trim tool to carefully prise out the plastic plugs that secure the back of the parcel shelf carpet in position. Behind this carpet there are a series of thirteen 10mm nuts that secure the base of the hood.

6. Undo all the 10mm nuts around the base of the back of the hood. These secure a long metal set plate in position and two shorter lengths at the sides. Remove all of them from the car. The back of the hood cannot be removed yet.

7. Check the condition of the three metal set plates removed in the last step. If they are tatty and corroded, clean them with a wire brush, wipe them down and then paint them. Use an aerosol paint that dries quickly.

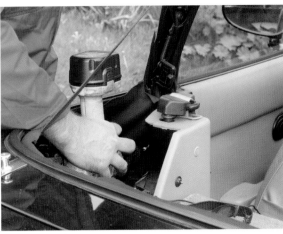

10. Undo the crosshead screws that secure the remains of the hood to the B-posts. You will also need to drill out a pop rivet close to the B-post, which secures what's left of the hood to the bodywork.

8. On hoods with a glass rear screen, the webbing that's fitted between the bars or hoops of the hood frame should be renewed, so cut the old ones off. Where the webbing is pop riveted to the hood frame, remove the rivets with an electric drill and 4mm bit.

11. The back of the hood can now be removed from the car. It may be riveted in the rain rail, in which case drill the heads off the rivets. However, leave the rain rail in position, as this will be reused.

9. Fit the new webbing in the same position on the hood frame as the old material. Use a pop rivet gun to secure the webbing to the original mounting points – make sure the old pop rivets have been removed.

12. The rubber seals over the tops of the door glass need to be removed to access some screws that hold the remains of the hood to the frame. Undo two crosshead screws, then prise the seal off the hood frame using a trim tool.

13. Look for a small crosshead screw close to the B-post when the hood is folded down. This secures the hood to the framework and needs to be undone to remove the remains of it.

16. Remove the part of the hood where each tensioner cable travels through. The tensioner cable doesn't usually need to be renewed, so leave it attached at the rear of the hood frame.

14. Undo the three crosshead screws that were concealed by the rubber seal removed in step 12. Once undone, remove the metal mounting plate, and the remains of the hood trapped by it will be released.

17. Fold the remains of the hood down flat, then undo the series of crosshead screws along the front. Once undone, remove the remains of the front section of the old hood and keep the metal strip.

15. At each front corner of the hood, look for a pop rivet that secures the front of each tensioner cable in position (there's one on each side). Drill out each pop rivet to release the cable at the front.

18. Look into the bodywork, just behind the B-posts on each side of the car, for a drain hole. It will probably be blocked, so poke a thin metal rod down it and pour some hot water through to remove any dirt.

Fitting the New Hood

1. Put the hood frame up, then take the new hood and loosely fit it over the rear so that the glass screen is somewhere in position. We'll start by fitting the hood to the hood frame.

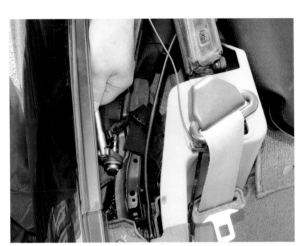

2. Refit the crosshead screw that was removed in step 13 of the previous section. It's threaded into the bottom of the B-post – make sure it's fitted through a clamp and the relevant part of the hood.

3. Fit a long cable tie to the ends of the two cable tensioners. Thread the cable ties through the channels in the side of the hood and pull them all the way through to, in turn, pull the cable tensioners.

4. With the cable tensioners fitted (remove the cable ties), pop rivet the ends to the front of the hood frame. The old pop rivets were drilled out in step 15 of the previous section.

5. Fit the hood over the frame where the metal strips and rubber seals were removed in steps 12 and 14 in the previous section. Refit these parts to the hood frame on both sides.

6. Pop rivet the hood to the base of the hood frame where it's secured to the B-post on each side of the car. The old pop rivet was drilled out in step 10 of the previous section.

7. Wrap the front of the hood around the front of the hood frame. Make sure the corners of the hood are straight and square, then refit the metal strip and crosshead screws removed in step 17 of the previous section.

10. From inside the car, feed the back of the hood over the mounting studs, then refit the three metal set plates and all of the 10mm nuts. Tighten them progressively to ensure the metal set plates clamp the hood.

8. Pieces of foam strip are supplied with the hood. Place them over the studs that secure the back of the hood. This helps to prevent water from leaking from the rain rail through the oversize holes and into the parcel shelf area.

11. Sit inside the car and test that the hood can easily be secured across the top of the windscreen. Also, check the hood is easy to detach at the front and to fold down. Test this out a few times.

9. Put the hood up and straighten it out. Feed the back of the hood down and into position, making sure the waterproof section is on the inside of the hood to ensure water doesn't get inside the car.

12. Fit the hood up, then get out of the car and check it sits flush at the rear and against the tops of the door glass. Any sign of looseness around the bodywork means that the hood has not been correctly fitted over all the studs.

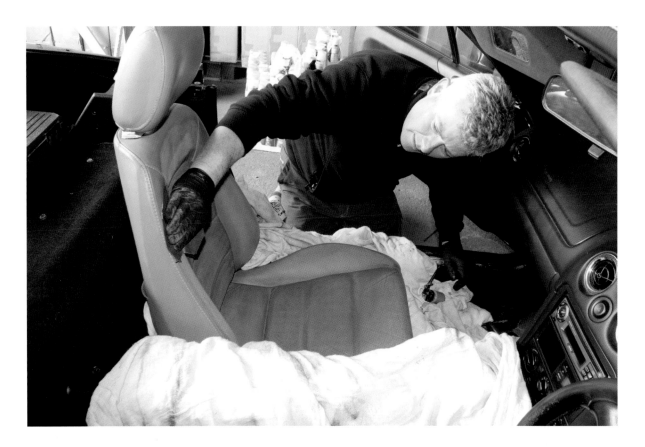

interior

SOUNDPROOFING

When the rose-tinted glasses are removed after driving an MX-5 several times, the rattles, squeaks and engine noise either become characterful or annoying. Such cars are rarely going to be as refined as a modern vehicle, but something can be done to make them more civilized. Panels that vibrate can be lined with a material that deadens the sound. Floors can be covered in thick matting to stop sounds transmitting through them. Engine bays can be lined with lead sandwich, an engine blanket and vibration-reduction material to help muffle noise. Even undersealing the wheelarches and underside of the floors can help.

The following steps show a Mk2 Mazda MX-5 being soundproofed by Noisekiller (www.noisekiller. co.uk). Before the car was soundproofed, there were numerous rattles and knocks that suggested the suspension was worn and several panels needed securing. Most of this was eradicated after the car

had been soundproofed, providing a noticeable reduction in panel rattles, vibrations and road and engine noise.

The work involved in soundproofing an MX-5 can be as simple or as complicated as you want it to be. It's worth removing the seats and carpets from the interior in order to fit soundproofing to the floors, propshaft tunnel and

TOOLBOX

- ◆ *Decorator's roller (small)*
- ◆ *Degreaser*
- ◆ *Ruler*
- ◆ *Scraper*
- ◆ *Screwdrivers*
- ◆ *Sharp craft knife*
- ◆ *Spanners/sockets: 10–17mm*
- ◆ *Tape measure*
- ◆ *Trim tools*

Time: 6–8 hours
On your own? Yes

rear bulkhead. In the engine bay, the underside of the aluminium bonnet can be soundproofed to help reduce vibrations and absorb engine noise. The boot can be stripped so you can line it in a material to reduce vibrations – the boot amplifies exhaust and road noise. A thicker boot mat can also be fitted to block sound.

Stripping the Interior

1. Soundproofing a vehicle is a good opportunity to strip the interior, clean it and check for corrosion. Start by removing the seats, which are usually secured with four 14mm bolts – two at the front and two at the rear.

2. If there are covers fitted over the tops of the sills, these will need to be removed before you can lift the carpets. Use a trim tool to carefully lever the covers off. They may be brittle and could easily break.

3. Undo the 17mm bottom seatbelt mounting bolt so you can lift up the carpet. Once undone, move the carpet out of the way, then refit the bolt, loosely fitting it for now to ensure you don't lose it.

4. The footrest in the driver's footwell can be removed to make it easier to lift the carpet and apply soundproofing material to the propshaft tunnel. This is secured with a couple of dome-headed 10mm nuts.

5. The centre console needs to be removed if you want to soundproof the propshaft tunnel. Remove the box inside the ashtray, then undo two crosshead screws. Undo more crosshead screws inside the lockable compartment.

6. Prise up the switch panel for the electric windows and disconnect the plug. Undo the retaining screws at the side of the centre console and unscrew the gear knob. You should now be able to lift off the centre console.

1. Two pieces of thick sound barrier can be fitted on each side of the floor. This is supplied pre-cut from Noisekiller and helps to reduce vibrations and block road noise. In the centre of the matting there is an open cell acoustic foam that absorbs airborne sounds.

7. The carpet for the floors and over the propshaft tunnel may be secured with some plastic plugs, which can be carefully released with a trim tool. Work around the carpet, making sure it isn't secured to any part of the car.

2. Remove the carpeting from the rear bulkhead and fit two large sections of self-adhesive barrier mat. This helps to reduce vibrations and block noise from the road and the differential. Make sure it's firmly stuck down by going over it with a decorator's roller.

8. Inspect the floors and check everything is dry. Remove any old soundproofing using a scraper. Dry anything that is wet and treat any corrosion before fitting the new soundproofing material.

3. The sides of the propshaft tunnel can also be covered in self-adhesive barrier mat. A large single piece can be fitted on the driver's side and three smaller pieces can be fitted on the passenger's side.

4. The top of the propshaft tunnel has room for three small strips of self-adhesive barrier mat. Do not cover over the mounting holes for the centre console. Once fitted, the carpets can be refitted and the interior reassembled.

3. Peel back the plastic waterproof sheeting to see where the barrier mat can be fitted inside the door. Use small pieces and see if they can be easily fed into position without sticking to everything.

Soundproofing the Doors

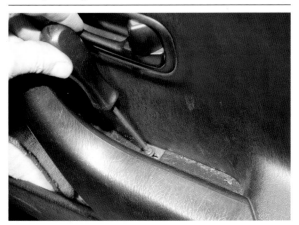

1. The insides of the doors can be soundproofed with self-adhesive barrier mat, so the door cards have to be removed. Start by undoing the securing screw inside the internal grab handle and behind the door handle.

4. After fitting a few pieces of barrier mat, make sure they are securely stuck down by running over them with a decorator's roller. Water will drip down the inside of the door, so the barrier mat must be secure.

2. There's another screw at the top of the grab handle, a plastic trim plug near the front of the door card, then several clips to release before the door card can be lifted off the door. Detach the speaker wiring.

Soundproofing the Boot

1. Remove all the contents of the boot, including the spare wheel, any tools, the carpets and moulded side trim (secured with plastic trim plugs). Dry out the boot if it's wet and treat any rust.

4. Fit a large piece of self-adhesive barrier mat in the floor of the spare wheel well. Use a decorator's roller to ensure all the barrier mat is stuck down. If the floor of the boot is wet, dry it out first.

2. A steel panel is fitted around the petrol tank filler neck. This can be removed to fit more soundproofing material, so undo the 10mm bolts that secure it, then carefully manoeuvre it out of the boot.

5. Small pieces of barrier mat can be fitted inside the rear wings. There's not much room to fit these. Tap the panels to see where the noise is generated, then trial fit a piece or two in position.

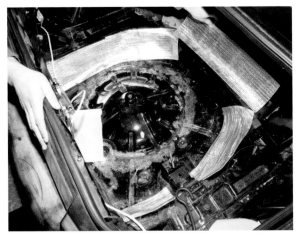

3. Trial fit several pieces of self-adhesive barrier mat around the walls of the spare wheel well. Don't stick them down until you have trial fitted all the pieces to ensure the area is fully covered.

6. Here's the boot area lined with self-adhesive barrier mat. Additional pieces have been fitted on the front and rear walls of the boot, plus the floor to the side of the spare wheel well.

7. Another area of the boot to be soundproofed is the underside of the boot lid. The single-skin areas can be covered in self-adhesive Vibrasorb, which helps to reduce panel vibration and absorb sounds.

2. Noisekiller use templates for cutting out the Vibrasorb and their other soundproofing materials, so all of the soundproofing material is supplied pre-cut for fitting into the MX-5.

8. The final piece of soundproofing for the boot consists of a large sheet of non-adhesive sound barrier. This can be fitted under the boot carpet and helps to reduce vibrations and block road and exhaust noise.

3. Trial fit the pieces of Vibrasorb to the underside of the bonnet to determine where each one needs to be secured. If a piece is a little too large to fit, it can be trimmed with a sharp knife.

Engine Soundproofing

1. The underside of the bonnet can be soundproofed in self-adhesive Vibrasorb to help reduce engine noise. First this area needs to be cleaned with a degreaser to remove any dirt and oil residue.

4. Peel off the backing paper from the Vibrasorb and fit each piece onto the single-skin sections of the bonnet. Use a decorator's roller to press the Vibrasorb down firmly and ensure it has stuck to the bonnet.

TOOLBOX

- ◆ **2mm drill bit**
- ◆ **Bradawl**
- ◆ **Electric drill**
- ◆ **Flat file**
- ◆ **Hacksaw blade**
- ◆ **Screwdrivers**
- ◆ **Trim tools**

CENTRE CONSOLE TROUBLE

The MX-5's centre console is secured to the top of the prop-shaft tunnel with several crosshead screws. It's a sophisticated design, incorporating a lockable compartment, a surround for the gear lever, an ashtray and the switches for the electric windows (if applicable).

Problems can arise with the centre console. The switches for the electric windows can fail, but these are straightforward to remove using a trim tool. The hinges for the console's lockable lid can break along the plastic edges. A second-hand lid or centre console can be expensive, but there is a cheaper solution, which is outlined as a step-by-step guide here, along with information on how to remove the centre console and extract the switches for the electric windows (more information on the electric windows is included later in this chapter).

Use a screwdriver, bradawl or trim tool to lever up the switches for the electric windows.

Centre Console Removal

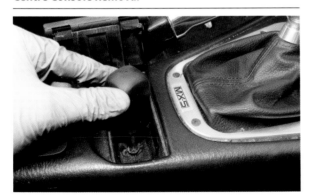

1. Lift the ashtray lid and remove the plastic compartment inside to reveal two crosshead screws that secure the centre console in position. Undo both of them.

Time: 1–2 hours
On your own? Yes

2. Open the lid for the centre console lockable compartment and look for a couple more crosshead screws to undo. The centre console cannot be removed yet.

3. Look along the sides of the centre console for some plastic screw caps. Prise off each cap to reveal a crosshead screw. Undo all of these to release the centre console.

4. Unscrew the gear knob, then try to lift the centre console upwards. Detach the wiring for the electric window switches (if fitted) and manoeuvre the gaiter over the gear lever.

Repairing a Broken Hinge

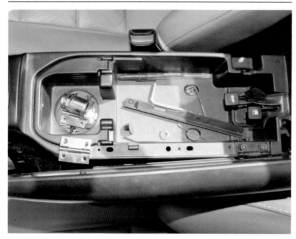

1. If the plastic hinge for the centre console's lockable compartment lid has broken, as shown here, it may be possible to fit a metal hinge from a DIY or hardware store.

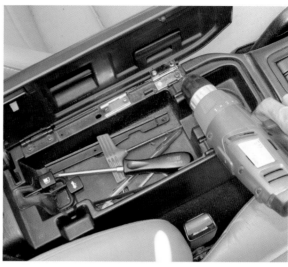

4. There are no mounting points on the underside of the lid, so pre-drill some holes using a 2mm drill bit. The lid isn't made from solid plastic, so the holes are easy to make.

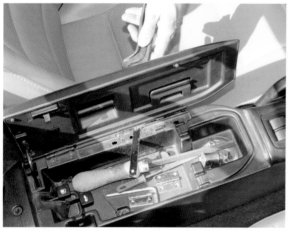

2. Cut off the lip on the side of the centre console, then file it down to make sure the new hinge is mounted flush. There should be enough space to do this without having to remove the lid.

5. Secure the new hinge to the underside of the lid with small grub screws. Check the lid can close and that it sits flush to the centre console.

3. The new hinge may be able to reuse some of the original mounting points for the plastic hinge that has broken off. Make new holes using a bradawl or a similar tool for making a hole.

6. These universal hinges were a bargain at less than £2, have remained secure for several years and now allow the centre console compartment to be used and locked.

FITTING A ROLL CAGE

There are a number of different types of roll cage that can be fitted inside an MX-5. Most of them are secured to the bodywork underneath the rear parcel shelf. In some cases a hood with a glass rear screen cannot be fitted (a plastic rear screen is required instead).

The following steps show a roll cage from Peterborough-based Ewens Sports Cars (also known as Fenspeed Motorsport) being fitted to a Mk2 MX-5; this can also be fitted into a Mk1.

The work involved in fitting a cage starts with removing the carpeting, sound-deadening material and metal panel that form the rear parcel shelf. Then you can see the bodywork where the cage is mounted. Some of the bodywork has to be cut and modified to be able to fit the cage, and after trial fitting it, several mounting holes need to be marked before removing the cage and drilling them out.

Once the cage has been fitted, you may discover the hood is a little more awkward to fit than usual. If this is the case, fit the hood as best as possible and expose it to sunlight to warm it up and stretch it.

So will a roll cage make a difference to the handling of an MX-5, or is it purely there for added peace of mind? There should be less scuttle shake and vibrations from the rear when driving over rough surfaces. The handling may feel firmer and the MX-5 should feel more sure-footed under hard cornering. The only trouble with uprating one aspect of the car's handling is that a new weak spot is discovered. So it probably won't be long before you're thinking about changing the coil springs, uprating the dampers or renewing the suspension bushes.

TOOLBOX

◆ **Airsaw or hacksaw**
◆ **Angle grinder or flat file**
◆ **Angled drill attachment from Machine Mart (part number 060220232)**
◆ **Chisel**
◆ **Drill with 4–10mm drill bits**
◆ **Hammer**
◆ **Ratchet strap**
◆ **Red marker pen**
◆ **Round file**
◆ **Spanners/sockets: 10–17mm and Torx T40**
◆ **Tin snips, jigsaw or similar to cut through plastic trim**
◆ **Trim tool remover**
◆ **Vice grips**

Time: 6–8 hours
On your own? Yes

1. The hood doesn't need to be removed to fit the roll cage, but the rear parcel shelf carpet and sound-deadening material does. First it has to be detached from the back of the hood by undoing a series of 10mm nuts.

2. If a wind deflector is fitted, it has to be removed and probably cannot be refitted. It's secured with a 10mm bolt and crosshead screw at each side, which are awkward to access as space is tight.

3. The carpet and sound-deadening material can now be completely removed from the MX-5. This can be re-trimmed and refitted if required, or discarded.

4. The plastic trim around the B-post has to be removed. First prise off the trim along the sills and the rubber seal that runs up the B-post. Undo two screws around the top of the B-post before unclipping the plastic trim.

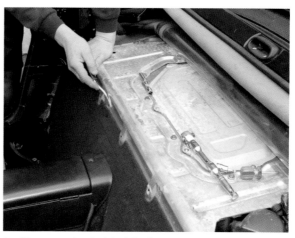

5. The carpeting behind the front seats has to be released to access the bolts for a panel behind and above it. Use a trim tool remover to release the plastic plugs that keep the carpet in place. Typical of their age, some of them may break.

6. The thin steel panel that covers part of the bulkhead and the rear parcel shelf is secured with several 10mm bolts. Undo all of them then remove the panel. It can be re-trimmed and refitted later if required.

7. Small pieces of sound deadening material can be removed and discarded. Look for wiring that is going to get in the way of fitting the roll cage. There may be a few plugs that need to be removed from their mounts or detached.

8. This 10mm bolt and the one to the left will obstruct the cage when it's fitted, so they have to be removed. The cage will be bolted to this panel and the one below it, improving their rigidity. The earth wire shown here also needs relocating.

11. The seatbelt's inertia reel needs to be removed to fit the cage, but will be refitted later. This is secured with one 10mm bolt at the top and a larger 17mm bolt below. The inertia reel can be suspended as it cannot be fully removed.

9. The lip on the panel shown here has to be removed in order to fit the cage. Cut a line down it, then chisel out the spot welds and use a pair of vice grips to waggle and eventually remove it. This must be done on both sides of the car.

12. Trial fit the cage using a ratchet strap to pull the sides together. Carefully ease the cage into position, taking care not to trap any wires. When it's correctly located, mark the mounting holes with a red marker pen, then remove the cage.

10. The top seatbelt mount needs to be removed, but will be refitted later once the cage has been fitted. There's one 17mm bolt to undo, which secures the top mount and has several washers and spacers to collect.

13. There are six M10 holes to drill on each side of the car. Start with pilot holes and use a right-angled adaptor (available from Machine Mart) as space is tight, then enlarge the holes with a round file. This step takes roughly one hour to complete.

14. Refit the cage and check all of the mounting bolts can be fitted; you may need to remove the cage and enlarge some of the holes. When all of the bolts are located, refit the seatbelt inertia reels and top mounts.

16. Refit all wiring, including any earth wires (new locations may be required). Finally, trim the B-post panels to ensure they can be fitted. Tin snips can be used to cut through the composite panels.

LEATHER RENOVATION

15. Eight of the cage's mounting bolts require spreader plates and locking nuts to be fitted from underneath the car. The remaining four bolts are fitted inside the car with washers and locking nuts. Fully tighten all fittings once they are in position.

The MX-5's seats before they were repaired. The leather is cracked and marked.

The restored seats look so much better. Applying more lacquer will give a shinier vinyl finish.

MX-5 leather seats can become cracked and scuffed over time, especially the outer side bolster of the driver's seat. Fortunately, this sort of damage can be repaired by filling the cracks with a glue and pigment and repainting the entire seat. It also helps to wash the leather thoroughly with a suitable cleaning product and gently scrub it with a nylon brush to help remove any engrained dirt.

Other leather-bound objects, such as the steering wheel, can become bleached by the sun. These can also be renovated using similar techniques to reviving leather seats.

DIY leather renovation kits are available from a wide range of specialists. The hardest part is finding a colour match for the leather. A straight black leather seat and steering wheel may not be too difficult, but a light brown leather seat, for example, isn't quite so straightforward.

The following steps show leather specialist Paul Gaskin from Leather Revive (www.LeatherRevive.co.uk) restoring the light brown leather seats in a Mk2 MX-5 and the black leather Nardi steering wheel.

TOOLBOX

- ◆ **Hairdryer**
- ◆ **Leather cleaning solution**
- ◆ **Leather restoration kit**
- ◆ **Masking tape**
- ◆ **Nylon nail brush**
- ◆ **Scotchbrite pad**
- ◆ **Spatula**
- ◆ **Wet and dry paper (P400)**

Time: 3–4 hours
On your own? Yes

1. Start by cleaning the seats with a nylon nail brush and some leather cleaning fluid. This helps to remove engrained dirt that will prevent the new paint/pigment from sticking to the leather.

3. Any deep marks that cannot be removed with the nylon brush or Scotchbrite can be removed with P400 grade wet and dry paper. The abrasive action of the wet and dry will leave a rough finish, but it will be covered with a pigment.

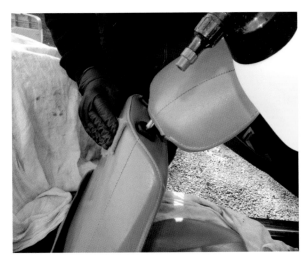

2. Don't be afraid to scrub the leather and use Scotchbrite pads with a leather cleaning fluid to remove stubborn marks. The scouring action of the Scotchbrite is more abrasive than the nylon brush.

4. Any areas of the seat that don't need to be treated, such as the recliner controls and other plastic parts, should be protected with masking tape to prevent them being discoloured with pigment and filler.

5. Scuff marks and cracks can be filled with a combination of leather glue and leather filler. This helps to build the leather back up. The glue helps the flexible filler to adhere to the leather. Allow it to dry before rubbing it down with wet and dry paper.

8. Some of the cracks in the seat may require a few coats of pigment. Pigment can also be applied as filler with a spatula. Applying the pigment this way helps to fill in the cracks.

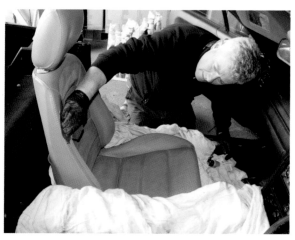

6. Skill and an eye for colour matching come in handy when mixing a pigment to match the colour of the MX-5's seats. Some kits can provide a colour match based on the model of the car or a colour sample.

9. Once the pigment has dried, you can see whether it has adequately covered the leather. If it has, rub all of it down with wet and dry to help key the finish for the final coat.

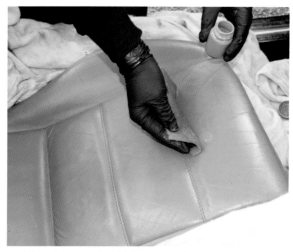

7. The pigment should be applied using a Scotchbrite pad, which helps to rub it gently into the leather. Difficult sections, such as piping, can be coloured using a small spatula that is available from craft shops.

10. The final coat can be sprayed on and consists of a mixture of pigment and lacquer. It helps to provide a sealed finish. Using more lacquer will give a shiny finish that looks more like vinyl, while less lacquer will produce more of a leather finish.

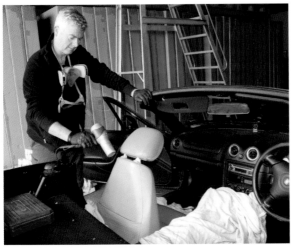

11. Dry the wet pigment and lacquer using a hairdryer (a heat gun can also be used). This helps to shorten the drying time and assess the results of the repair.

2. Scrub the dirt out of the steering wheel using a nylon nail brush with some leather cleaning fluid. The dirt will prevent the colour that needs to be added to the steering wheel from sticking to it.

12. If you are not happy with the results, try warming up the filler and pigment, and then mould it with your fingers to try to reshape it. Leave the seats for 12 hours before using them.

3. More dirt can be removed using a Scotchbrite pad with leather cleaning fluid. It's not just dirt that needs to be removed. Silicone-based cleaners also need to come off, as they don't help when it comes to applying a repair colour.

Restoring a Leather Steering Wheel

1. This MX-5's leather-bound steering wheel has been bleached by the sun, so most of the finish has disappeared from around the top of it. However, it can be made to look as good as new with a little renovation.

4. The steering wheel's leather needs to be keyed before the black pigment can be applied. This will help the pigment to stick to it, so rub over it with 400 grade wet and dry paper.

5. Apply black pigment using a clean piece of Scotchbrite. Rub it into the leather, making sure it is applied evenly.

6. Use a hairdryer to dry the black pigment. It can be left to dry naturally if time allows; otherwise, artificial drying is acceptable.

7. Once the pigment has dried, a final coat of pigment and lacquer should be sprayed onto the steering wheel. The lacquer helps to produce a sealed finish. Protect the dashboard with a thick sheet.

8. A final run over with the hairdryer helps the pigment and lacquer to dry quickly. Check the finish to ensure you are satisfied with the restored steering wheel.

9. The restored steering wheel looks like real leather again. It should be left to dry fully for at least 24 hours.

WINDOW WINDER TROUBLE

The MX-5's door windows can struggle to move up and down, which is often caused initially by a lack of routine maintenance mixed with wear and tear over years of use.

Remove the door card and peel back the waterproof sheet to access the channels that guide the door glass up and down.

Spray WD40 down the felt or rubber guide channels. These can become dry and restrict the movement of the door glass.

The channels that guide the edges of the door glass as it moves up and down can get dry, causing excessive resistance for the window winder mechanism. Try spraying light grease or spreading multi-purpose grease down the channels to see if this helps. It's often easier to do this by removing the door card and peeling back the plastic waterproof sheeting. The felt guides for the door glass can restrict the movement of the window, so spray something like WD40 inside them.

All the mounting points for the window winder mechanism must be secure to avoid any movement and the risk of the glass jamming, so remove the door card and check all the nuts and bolts that keep it secure are not loose.

If the door glass moves too far up or doesn't move enough, then it may be possible to fix the problem by adjusting the position of the window stops. These can be found by removing the door card and looking near the top of the door. There are two of them on each door and they are secured with a 10mm bolt – slacken the bolt and adjust the position of the stop.

In the case of electric windows, a blown fuse is often the cause of one not working at all, and the correct starting point for diagnosing the problem. The MX-5 has individual fuses for each electric window, so don't overlook the fuses if one electric window isn't working. There is also a relay

for the electric windows, usually sited next to the fusebox, so locate it and check it clicks when operating the window switch.

If the fuses are all intact, then check the wiring to the motor inside the door. Remove the door card and look inside the door for the wiring to the window regulator motor. Make sure the wiring is securely connected. Trace it back through the door, checking it isn't damaged.

The next stage is to look at the electric window switch. Prise it out of its housing and use a multimeter to check the voltage supply to the switch that operates the electric window. You will need to switch on the ignition to test this. If there's no reading, look again at the fuses and relay switch.

If you still can't get the electric window working, the next solution is to remove the window regulator (motor and mechanism) and either test it separately by connecting it to a battery (use thick wires and keep your fingers away from the moving mechanism), or source a working second-hand replacement. This is a more common solution, so the following steps show how to remove an electric window regulator and renew it.

Testing an electric window regulator is feasible, but use thick wires and keep your fingers away from any moving parts.

Renewing an Electric Window Regulator

TOOLBOX

- ◆ *Light and multi-purpose grease*
- ◆ *Pliers*
- ◆ *Screwdrivers*
- ◆ *Sockets/spanners: 10–14mm*
- ◆ *Trim tools*

Time: 1–2 hours
On your own? Yes

Adjusting the position of this door stop will alter how far up the door glass travels.

1. Remove the door card by prising out any plastic trim plugs and undoing several screws. Once removed, peel back the waterproof sheeting and remove anything else that's in the way, such as polystyrene sound-proofing.

4. With the base of the glass not secured to the window regulator, and the stops removed from inside the door, the glass can now be lifted out. This can be quite awkward. Be careful not to drop the glass and store it safely aside.

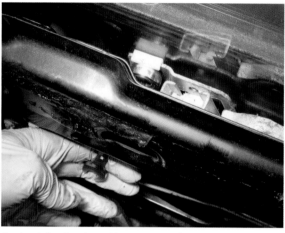

2. Look for the three 10mm screws that secure the base of the door glass to the window regulator. If the window can be wound down, this may provide better access. Otherwise, squeeze a spanner in to undo them. Disconnect the battery.

5. You will need all the space you can get to manoeuvre the window regulator out, so remove parts you don't want to get damaged, such as the door speakers. Undo the crosshead screws that secure the speakers to the doors, lift them out and disconnect the two wires.

3. Remove the two window stops fitted near the top of the door, which prevent the door glass being pushed too far up and also allow for adjustment of the height of the glass. These stops are each secured with a 10mm bolt.

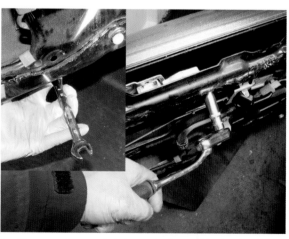

6. There are two metal channels that guide the door glass up and down – one of them is part of the window regulator mechanism. They are secured to the door with 12mm nuts. Undo all of them to ensure the window regulator can be removed.

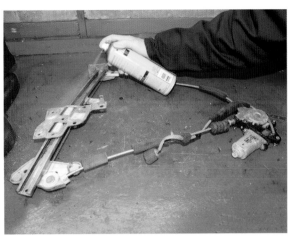

7. The window regulator's motor is secured to the door with three 10mm nuts. Undo all of them. The window regulator should now feel loose inside the door, and you may find a few more nuts and bolts to undo.

10. After removing the window regulator, you may find it can be repaired, especially if a cable has snapped. When you're ready to refit it or fit another one, lubricate the moving parts with some light grease.

8. Trace the wiring for the window regulator and detach any fittings that keep it secure inside the door. These fittings are important because they ensure the door glass doesn't foul the wiring when it moves up and down.

11. Before fitting the window regulator inside the door, trial fit it from the outside to see how it needs to be positioned. Note which parts can easily get damaged, such as the rods for the door lock and handle.

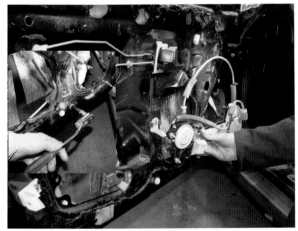

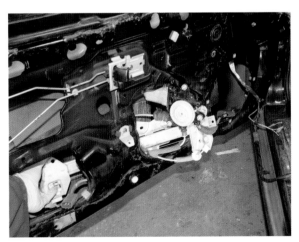

9. The quarter-light strut will obstruct the removal of the window regulator, so undo its two 10mm bolts to allow it to be moved aside and the window regulator's channels fed behind it. Manoeuvre the window regulator motor out of the door.

12. Carefully manoeuvre the window regulator inside the door. Refit all of the mounting nuts and bolts, but don't fully tighten any of them until they have all been fitted. Reconnect the wiring and battery to test the regulator works.

STEREO UPGRADES

Renewing the Head Unit

The MX-5's stereo is mounted in the centre console, in the middle of the dashboard. There are a number of alternative aftermarket stereos that can be fitted here. Removal of the old stereo is straightforward, often only requiring a pair of removal tools, which can be bought from most car audio specialists and general motor factors.

One of the most popular stereo upgrades for most vehicles is to fit an amplifier, which often improves the sound quality when compared to a standard stereo set-up of a head unit and speakers. However, the MX-5's interior is so small that there's little space to fit an amplifier, and also little point in improving the sound quality for such a small cabin. Instead, a good-quality head unit is often sufficient – and some have built-in amplification equipment to help improve sound quality.

3. Before the new head unit is fully fitted, connect its wiring and test it to make sure it works. You may need to enter a code to activate it.

1. The old head unit can usually be removed using a pair of stereo removal tools, which consist of flat pieces of metal with the ends upturned for extra leverage.

4. If a new mounting cage is supplied with the new head unit, you may want to replace the existing cage. Lock tabs around the cage will need to be released in order for you to remove it.

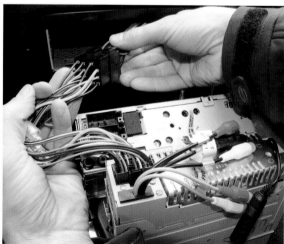

2. Detach the multi-plug on the back of the old head unit. You may need an adaptor plug to connect to the new head unit, which may be included. Otherwise, these are available from a car audio shop.

5. After fitting the new head unit, test all of its functions and features. Make sure the head unit is secure and cannot be removed without the removal tools described in step 1.

New Speakers

The MX-5's door speakers can be upgraded with a wide range of aftermarket items. The main speakers that are fitted to the front bottom corners of each door are located in their own plastic housings, so try to use a speaker that has exactly the same dimensions. This will ensure the new speaker is straightforward to fit, requiring no modifications to the existing plastic housing.

1. Remove the door panels. Each one is secured with a selection of crosshead screws and plastic trim plugs. The trim plugs can be released with a small flat-blade screwdriver, and they may break off.

2. The original door speakers are secured with crosshead screws to a plastic housing. Try removing the speaker on its own, although you may have to remove the housing at the same time. Detach the two wires.

3. The photograph here shows a standard MX-5 speaker secured to the housing with sealant; the two need to be separated using a sharp knife.

4. New wiring connections may be required to ensure the two standard speaker wires can be connected to the back of the new speakers. Secure the new speaker to the standard plastic housing, then switch on the car's stereo to test it.

projects

RESTORATION: HOW TO STRIP A SHELL

The Mazda MX-5 is probably one of the easiest cars to fully dismantle, whether you are conducting a thorough restoration or scrapping a car and collecting as many parts as possible to reuse.

In brief, underneath the MX-5 there are front and rear subframes with a propshaft and power plant frame (PPF) linking the two. The front subframe holds the engine, gearbox, brakes and front suspension, whereas the rear subframe retains the diff, driveshafts, rear suspension and brakes. There are just fourteen nuts and bolts that secure the front and rear subframes to the underside of the body, which, when undone along with several hoses, plug connectors and the nuts for the tops of the suspension struts, allow the bodyshell to be lifted up and away. The parts that are left on the floor look similar to a rolling chassis.

Dismantling a Mazda MX-5 is best completed with a two-post ramp, although it is possible to use an engine crane to raise the bodyshell.

TOOLBOX

- ◆ *Chisel (blunt)*
- ◆ *Drainage tray*
- ◆ *Hammer*
- ◆ *Penetrating fluid*
- ◆ *Pry bar*
- ◆ *Screwdrivers*
- ◆ *Sockets/spanners: 8–24mm*
- ◆ *Transmission jack*
- ◆ *Trolley jack*
- ◆ *Two-post ramp or engine crane*

Time: 4–6 hours
On your own? Yes

1. It's worth draining the fluids from the rear diff (24mm bolt), gearbox (24mm bolt) and engine oil sump (17/19mm sump plug) to avoid spills when dismantling.

4. Remove the catalytic converter, then detach and remove the rear section of the exhaust. If a rear brace is fitted, undo two 17mm bolts and drop it down to help remove the exhaust.

2. The coolant can be drained from the radiator by unscrewing the cap from the top of the radiator to release any pressure, then releasing the drain in the bottom of the radiator.

5. Undo the 12mm bolts for the front anti-roll bar clamps. The anti-roll bar doesn't need removing, just its clamps undoing, which are secured to the bodywork.

3. Remove the plastic undertrays from underneath the engine. Most of these are secured with a series of 10mm nuts and bolts. Some of them will probably shear off, so spray all of them with penetrating fluid first.

6. The front and rear brake flexi-hoses need disconnecting. If they are going to be renewed, cut through them. Also, cut through or detach the OSR brake pipe where it's attached to the bodywork.

7. If a rear brace is fitted, remove it. The brace is secured with a series of 17mm bolts, which will need spraying with penetrating fluid to reduce the risk of them shearing.

8. Detach the front to rear wiring loom from inside the propshaft tunnel. It's secured with a series of plastic clips and 10mm bolts.

9. Unscrew the speedo cable from the bottom of the gearbox and detach the wiring for the reverse sensor.

10. Remove the induction pipework. Detach the radiator's top and bottom hoses and its electric fan wiring, and remove the radiator from inside the engine bay – it's secured with two 12mm or 14mm nuts or bolts.

11. Remove the battery. From inside the engine bay, disconnect the wiring to the starter motor and alternator. Detach the plugs and earth point from the front of the engine and move the loom away.

12. Detach all coolant, fuel and breather pipes from the engine that are attached to the bodywork.

15. Spray penetrating fluid over the four 19mm nuts that secure the front subframe to the chassis legs, then slacken them. Don't fully remove them yet.

13. The steering column needs to be disconnected from the steering rack. Undo the two 12mm bolts for the UJ coupling, then undo the 14mm bolts for the two steering rack clamps.

16. Slacken the four 14mm bolts that secure the rear of the front subframe to the underside of the body. Do not remove them yet.

14. Use a hammer and blunt chisel or pry bar to separate the steering column from the steering rack. Once detached, refit the bolts for the steering rack's two clamps.

17. At the rear, undo the six 19mm nuts and bolts that secure the rear subframe to the underside of the body. Position a trolley or gearbox jack under the rear diff, then remove these fixings and all the nuts and bolts in steps 15 and 16.

20. Remove the centre console, secured with a series of 10mm bolts or screws, and undo four 12mm bolts that secure the gear lever surround to the propshaft tunnel.

18. Lower the car to the ground so it's sitting on its wheels. From under the bonnet, undo the two 14mm nuts that secure the top of the suspension coilovers to the body-work.

21. Carefully raise the bodyshell and make sure the front and rear subframes, with the propshaft attached between them, are left on the ground. Push down on the tops of the front struts to help release them.

19. From inside the boot, remove a metal shield around the filler pipework (secured with a 10mm bolt), then undo the two 14mm nuts for the top of the strut and the same on the other side.

22. As the bodyshell is raised, look out for any wires or hoses that may be caught or still attached. Don't go underneath the vehicle to detach anything, especially if the subframes haven't dropped down.

CASE STUDY: ELECTRIC MX-5 CONVERSION

Mitchell Yow from Torque Trends in the USA has converted a Mazda MX-5 to run on an electric motor. He wanted a rear-wheel-drive independent suspension car that would demonstrate his company's ev-Torque Box. During the autumn of 2013 a car was found and donated to the project by his late stepson Joshua, just before his passing. It was a 1999 MX-5 that had almost 200,000 miles on it, but was in pretty good shape. It had been repainted but had never been seriously damaged and had no major rust.

Mitchell had been involved in many electrification projects, mainly concerned with the drivetrain. This project was the first conversion where his team was responsible for everything from the front to rear bumper. Being a huge

Tesla fan, especially of the Tesla Roadster, he wanted to follow in their footsteps so he chose a 150kW, three-phase AC induction motor.

The main components for an electric power conversion are a motor; controller; on-board charger; a DC to DC convertor to drop pack voltage down to 13v for powering lights and accessories; a battery pack and battery management system; and gearing to multiply the motor's torque.

The parts that were not required from the MX-5 included the engine and all of its ancillaries, the entire exhaust system, the emissions equipment, the fuel system including the fuel tank, the four-speed automatic gearbox and even the hood and frame (Mitchell lives in a very sunny part of the USA).

Mitchell and his team officially started the project in December 2013. The electrification took approximately three months of part-time work. They also did a complete restoration with modifications to the body, chassis and interior, so the entire project took approximately six months.

Some electric motor conversions are mated to a standard manual gearbox, but this wasn't necessary in this case. However, it is necessary to fit a reduction gearbox. An electric motor makes nearly full torque at 1rpm and has a very broad torque band, so there is no need for a multi-speed transmission. Installing a single-speed reduction gearbox saves weight, eliminates unnecessary power loss and is thus more efficient, and to an electric car that means increased range and performance.

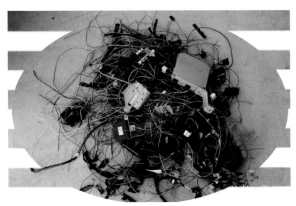

The old wiring loom is long and complicated, but thankfully not required.

ABOVE AND BELOW: Taking a standard 140bhp 1.8-litre Mk2 MX-5 with an automatic gearbox, Mitchell stripped the shell and had it painted, overhauled the suspension and brakes and rebuilt them with Bilstein coilovers and Wilwood brakes.

AC motor and ev-torque box joined together.

The rearmost battery pack is installed in the boot.

The reduction gearbox is manufactured by Mitchell's company and is called the ev-Torque Box. It reduces the speed (shaft rpm) but increases the motor's torque. For example, in his electric-powered MX-5, a single-speed 2:1 ratio is used, so when the motor is spinning at 10,000rpm, the output shaft is only turning at 5,000rpm but the motor's torque is double. The motor produces about 260Nm of torque, so with the reduction or multiplication factor, there's 520Nm available.

When it came to calculating how many batteries would be needed, Mitchell explains: 'We were creating a go-fast car, so we went with the maximum voltage specified by the motor manufacturer. In our case that was 360 volts nominal.'

A staggering one hundred 3.6v, 60amp lithium cells are spread throughout the car in three different battery boxes. This is commonly called a traction pack. The battery boxes are made from 6061 aluminium. Working with a team from Arizona State University, the car was laid out using computer aided design software (CAD) to determine the exact locations for the three battery boxes and thus retain the MX-5's excellent balance and handling characteristics.

Mitchell admits that it took a lot of time to find the right high-performance batteries. He wanted a lightweight battery that had the ability to release its stored energy quickly. He eventually found the batteries in China. They are stainless steel clad, weigh only 3.2lb each and have a special chemistry for quick release of energy – referred to as a C rating.

The parcel shelf and petrol tank area now houses a selection of lithium batteries.

So how does the car drive now on electric power? Mitchell explains:

The car has a lower centre of gravity, has gained 40lb and about 60 horsepower over the stock MX-5. It handles better, accelerates faster, is more fun to drive and will never waste time or money at the fuel pump again. In fact our MX-5 is charged from our 5kW rooftop solar system, making it a true zero emissions vehicle. Add to that the fact that it was converted from an existing car, this gives it the lowest carbon footprint of any car on the road today, bar none!

The ev-Torque Box installed in the MX-5's transmission tunnel.

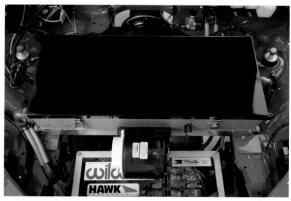

Under the bonnet there's no engine, but an AC motor controller and 15C NMC battery pack.

KIT CARS

The MX-5 has long been a popular donor car within the kit car industry. At first, its twin-cam engine, in-line manual gearbox and rear-wheel-drive configuration were transplanted into several Lotus Seven re-creations, and some of these were equipped with turbochargers and superchargers. Soon many other donor components from the MX-5 were used, including the steering, hubs and brakes. The advantage of using an MX-5 as the basis for a kit car such as a Lotus Seven-styled creation is that it is simple to strip the donor car and build up the new vehicle. It's feasible to complete all of the work in a single garage, providing large objects such as the unwanted MX-5 bodyshell are removed at the right time. Building up the new kit car can be completed with the chassis supported on axle stands at first, before the suspension, uprights, hubs and brakes are fitted, and it can be rolled around on its wheels.

The MNR VortX was one of the first Lotus Seven-styled kit cars to adopt the MX-5 as a single donor.

An MX-5 twin-cam engine sits neatly under the bonnet of most Lotus Seven-styled kit cars, including this MNR VortX.

Many popular kit cars that were formerly Ford Sierra based started to follow suit and adopt the MX-5 donor route. And new MX-5 based kit cars soon started to emerge. Some of the best known include the Healy Enigma that first appeared in 2011, which is intended to be a modern-looking Austin Healey. This initially adopted Mk1 and Mk2 MX-5 donor components before progressing to the Mk3, although the Mk2 option is still available.

The Mk1 and Mk2 MX-5 based Healy Enigma uses the donor car's front and rear rolling subframes, which are connected together with the propshaft and aluminium framework (PPF, or power plant frame). A substantial steel chassis is bolted on top of this assembly, which includes 1.5mm-thick sheet steel for the floors and a box-section gearbox and propshaft tunnel. MX-5 doors are hinged onto the chassis and the lower outer skin modified to change their appearance. The hood, glass and windscreen are also reused.

The Healy Enigma first appeared in 2011, based on many parts from the Mk1 or Mk2 MX-5.

The Enigma's bodywork is constructed from GRP and consists of a front and rear body tub, a windscreen surround, front and rear bumpers, sill in-fills and a section at the rear to allow the MX-5's hood to be reused. Estimated build time for an Enigma once the donor components are ready is around 250 hours.

One of the biggest range of MX-5-based kit cars has been created by Stuart Mills of Mills Extreme Vehicles. The most successful has been the budget-priced Exocet, which is a no-frills exoskeletal kit car that uses pretty much all of the MX-5 donor vehicle apart from the bodywork, glass, hood and lights. In brief, a metal chassis or framework is bolted

An MX-5 minus its bodyshell looks like this, making it ideal for a range of kit car projects.

MEV Exocet is tremendous fun to drive and very straightforward to build.

on top of the MX-5's front and rear rolling subframes to form the new vehicle. This approach to building a kit car has been very successful because most people can understand what's involved and quickly see how they can do it themselves. In the case of the MEV Exocet, it's also cheap.

There have been several other MEV creations based on the same approach as the Exocet, but with more bodywork, including the more practical Mevster, which has a windscreen, roof and doors. For the classic kit car market, there's the Replicar, which resembles the Aston Martin DBR1. MX-5 fans may remember the Superlight prototype from Mazda, which appeared at the Goodwood Festival of Speed in 2010 – MEV have created their own version.

The MEV Replicar resembles the Aston Martin DBR1 and is based on the Mk1 or Mk2 MX-5.

Over in the USA there are several more MX-5 based kit cars available, including the Catfish, which adopts a similar approach to MEV, using the subframes and mechanical components but not reusing the bodywork. Instead, the bodywork is constructed from GRP with carbon fibre reinforcements.

The speedster looks of the US Catfish conceal Mk1 or Mk2 MX-5 donor components under the new GRP bodywork.

Building a kit car isn't for everyone, especially if you don't want to strip a donor vehicle or get involved with building a car from a bare chassis. Fortunately, there is another solution that still falls within the remit of a kit car based on the MX-5: a panel kit. MEV's X5 is one such example, which sees a Mk1 or Mk2 MX-5 redecorated in GRP panelling to transform it into a coupé. Tribute Automotive have produced a similar panel kit, which loosely re-creates a Ferrari 250 GTO from a Mk1 or Mk2 MX-5.

MEV X5 is a panel kit that transforms a Mk1 or Mk2 into a coupé.

Panel kits are usually designed around donor vehicles where the majority of standard panels can be removed. The BMW Z3 is a perfect donor vehicle because all of its exterior panels can be unbolted, allowing new panels to be bolted or bonded in position. Sadly, the MX-5 isn't quite as flexible, so new panels often have to be bonded over the old steel parts, making the resulting car heavier and wider.

MX250 from Tribute Automotive re-creates the Ferrari 250 GTO with panels bonded onto a Mazda MX-5.

Case Study: Kit Car Build and Turbo Conversion

Roadrunner Racing's SR2 kit car uses many of the mechanical components from the MX-5.

Digital designer Tom Maffey admits he'd hardly done anything with cars when he embarked on the build of his MX-5-based MEV Exocet kit car.

'Having no tools, no knowledge and no experience was part of the original reason why I wanted to build the car in the first place,' he explains. 'I am an avid car and motor sport fan but had no knowledge, apart from some basics of how they worked mechanically. I find I learn best by jumping in and getting it wrong.'

Tom spent twelve months between May 2012 and 2013 building the Exocet seen here. First he found a 1.8-litre 1994 Mazda MX-5 as a donor vehicle, which, as he recalls, 'had been sat on a driveway for six months and a forecourt before that for one year.'

With a price tag of a mere £300, this Mk1 MX-5 was an ideal donor for an Exocet build.

It was mechanically sound but had one of the age-old problems with the Mk1 MX-5 – rusting rear sills. It can be an expensive job to sort as there are many MOT failures with this issue, he says. 'However, as the body was going to be scrapped I was not too worried about this. After a check to see if the rust had spread to any of the rear subframes and that the engine ran well, I purchased it there and then.'

The unroadworthy MX-5 was trailered home to Tom's garage, where, as he admits, 'I did not even have a socket set to start taking it apart.'

Once armed with the necessary tools, he got stuck in but found many of the nuts and bolts had seized, particularly the lower subframe bolts that secure the body. Luckily, there was always a solution.

'The best tool I bought was a three-foot-long breaker bar and a can of WD40,' he remarks.

The underneath of a Mazda MX-5 minus its bodyshell. The complete rolling assembly is used in the Exocet.

Following MEV's recommended method of removing the MX-5 body with an engine hoist, Tom hit a bit of a problem.

'I was not able to lift it high enough due to the roof supports in the garage,' he says. 'I therefore enlisted some help from family and friends and four of us lifted the shell by hand onto the trailer to be taken to the scrapyard.'

With the MX-5 bodyshell removed and a pair of rolling subframes with a connecting brace and propshaft remaining, the Exocet's round tube spaceframe-style chassis is bolted on top of this assembly. Unfortunately, Tom found it wasn't quite so straightforward to line up all the mounting points.

'It was the engine subframe that was the most problematic. The two mounting points had splayed outwards and away from the engine, either over time or when I removed the body. I therefore got a rope and ratchet system, as well as a neighbour who built custom trikes, to physically pull the subframe back together while I dropped in the bolts.'

MX-5 underbody components installed in the Exocet chassis.

Once the new chassis had been bolted on top of the MX-5 subframes, it was a matter of fitting the steering column, wiring in the electrics and fitting the exterior bodywork.

'I had a problem with the electrics due to my last involvement with them being ten years ago at school, and all knowledge I did have, had rapidly faded away,' he confesses. Those school lessons soon came back, but one particular gremlin took a lot of time to fix.

'My MX-5 had an aftermarket alarm and immobilizer that I needed to remove. However, once I did, the car no longer started. I then spent the best part of two weeks in the evenings trailing and testing each of the wires in the loom to locate the problem. It turned out I had disconnected one wire from the alarm loom and spliced it into the wrong connection.'

When it came to fitting the panels on the Exocet, these consist of a GRP bonnet, wings and rear cover, plus an optional pair of aluminium side panels.

'The panels were nice and simple to fit,' says Tom. 'I settled on aero catches for the bonnet, and after getting the PVC Foamex side panels completely wrong the first time (I cut the panel completely the wrong size), I luckily replaced it with some stock we keep at work.'

Work in progress. Aluminium floors and some GRP panels fitted.

of years, and providing the boost is kept at a realistically low level, most specialists have found the internals of the engine don't need to be uprated. Power outputs from a standard 1.6- or 1.8-litre MX-5 engine range from around 100 to just under 140bhp. Turbocharging will break most engines past the 200bhp barrier and 250bhp appears to be the agreed safety limit before the state of the internals is threatened.

One aspect of the build that Tom always intended to complete was to fit a turbocharger.

'My aim was to build a 350–400bhp per tonne track car for less than £10k,' he explains, knowing full well that such a target required either forced induction or an expensive and modified engine. However, his first aim was to complete the Exocet and get it through the IVA test before embarking on a turbo conversion.

'As this was the plan from day one there were certain decisions I made during the original build to pre-empt this future conversion. For instance, when I had a custom exhaust made by a local fabricator, I had it made with a 2.5in internal diameter to accommodate the future breathability of the turbo. I also resisted the urge to buy new manifolds or things I would have to replace at a later date to save on cost.'

Once the Exocet had passed the IVA in May 2013, Tom drove it for the summer and covered roughly 3,000 miles.

'I mainly wanted to make sure the car was mechanically sound before I started fettling with the engine,' he explains.

Turbo and supercharger conversion kits for Mazda MX-5 twin-cam engines have been available for a number

The Subaru WRX turbo is limited to 11psi to produce 234bhp at the rear wheels.

The Mk1 MX-5 1.8-litre twin-cam is reliable and robust enough to withstand a turbo conversion.

Tom sourced a turbo from a Subaru WRX, which was fitted to a custom-made steel manifold created by an MX5Nutz forum member called William (Sturovo). The air intake for the turbo is directed through a front-mounted intercooler that's available as an aftermarket upgrade for the Mk1 Seat Leon.

With the MX-5 engine using forced induction, the standard ECU was ditched for a Megasquirt system to fine-tune the fuelling. Further upgrades to the fuelling include four 425cc Yellow Top RX-8 injectors, a GM air temperature sensor attached to the intake system and an Innovate LC-2 wideband O2 sensor that replaces the standard Mazda lambda sensor.

'The turbo parts were very simple to fit with no major problems,' says Tom, who at the same time renewed the fuel lines from the filler neck to the fuel rail, replacing the rubber hoses with Teflon braided steel and converting the standard fuel rail to a dual-feed configuration.

I spent lots of time reading and researching to find out how other people have adapted the engines and what they have done to get my desired results. I therefore knew exactly what I was going to do, with all the parts bought and sat in the garage before I picked up any tools.

One aspect of the turbo conversion where Tom called in the experts was mapping the ECU. For this, he turned to Bailey Performance near Telford, and he has nothing but praise for their specialist knowledge. With the turbo running at 11psi of boost, there's an impressive 234bhp at the rear wheels and around 260ft lb of torque with a very flat power curve.

With so much extra power on tap, the suspension on this Exocet has been mildly uprated with Gaz Gold Pro coilovers, adjustable drop links and anti-roll bars all round. The brakes are deemed adequate, although EBC Green Stuff pads have recently been fitted.

So what does Tom think of his turbocharged Exocet and is it any better than when the engine was naturally aspirated?

The car before was great to drive. It was lively and a fun B-road toy; very similar to a standard MX-5 but a little lighter on its feet. With the turbo it is completely different. It now has all the same characteristics as the old car but with the added bonus of over double the original horsepower.

Having driven high-performance production cars, including a Ferrari F430, Porsche 911 turbo and an Ariel Atom, he finds his Exocet is noticeably quicker than all bar the Atom.

'Coming close to 400bhp per tonne, it launches itself off the line without any holding back and won't even struggle to accelerate if cruising at 40mph in fifth gear, immediately causing you to strain your neck and focus on the horizon,' he enthuses.

Tom is equally impressed with the Exocet's handling:

It's truly an outstanding car with the turn into a corner showing no signs of understeer and only as much oversteer as you will get carried away with. I have not found a point yet where the car has reached its limit before I have. It is a great car to drive but does require you to sit down and catch your breath afterwards.

index

RELATED TITLES FROM CROWOOD

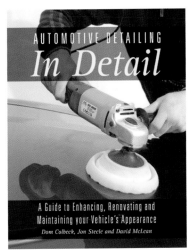
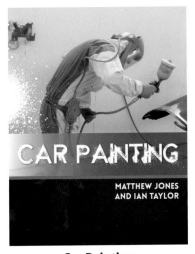
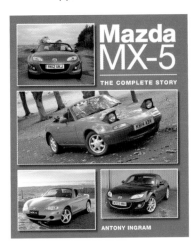
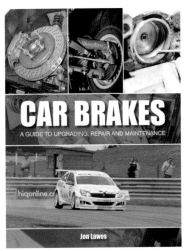
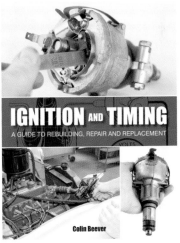